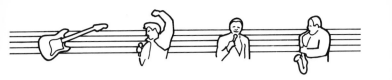

CHART BEATS

Dave McAleer

GUINNESS PUBLISHING

ACKNOWLEDGEMENTS

Many thanks to all the numerous music trivialists and writers whose works I have read and studied over the last 35 years. Very special thanks to Billie Gordon and Barry Lazell for their work and input. Thanks also to Alan Jones and Paul Grein who have helped to make music trivia less trivial.

Thanks to London Features International for the pictures in this book.

,

Project Editor: Honor Head
Assistant Editor: Paola Simoneschi
Design and Layout: Michael Morey
Cover Design: Amanda Ward
Picture Editor: Alex Goldberg

Published in Great Britain by Guinness Publishing Ltd,
33 London Road, Enfield, Middlesex

Typeset in Century Old Style and Futura by
Ace Filmsetting Ltd, Frome, Somerset
Printed and bound in Great Britain by
The Bath Press, Bath, Avon

'Guinness' is a registered trademark of Guinness Publishing Ltd

A catalogue record for this book is available from the British Library

ISBN 0-85112-964-1

The right of Dave McAleer to be identified as Author of this Work has been asserted in accordance with the Copyright, Design & Patents Act 1989.

AUTHOR

Dave McAleer began studying records and music charts in his pre-teen years in the mid-50s. He spent 25 years working in the record business on both sides of the Atlantic running companies, heading labels, working in A&R, promotion and marketing and has discovered many acts and helped many records chart. He has one of the world's largest collections of music publications and has written on all types of popular music for various magazines as well as having had several music books published. In 1976 he started the 'Music Business Trivia League' – the industry quiz league which preceded all the radio and TV music quiz games.

AUTHOR'S RECORD BREAKERS

He started the first Northern Soul label **Pye Disco Demand** and put Wigan on the chart map when he renamed the **Chosen Few** as **Wigan's Chosen Few** in 1975 . . . He started the first major record company disco department in the UK and sent out the first 'white label' records . . . He released the first rap record in the UK ('Rappers Delight' by the **Sugarhill Gang** in 1979) . . . He put together the first chart record including 'samples' from other records with 'Calibre Cuts' by the fictitious **Calibre Cuts** on his **Calibre** label in 1980 . . . In 1982 he gave award winning producer/mixer **Paul Oakenfold** his first studio job re-mixing the **Peech Boys** 'Don't Make Me Wait' on his **TMT** label, and he edited 'Planet Rock' by **Afrika Bambaata & the Soul Sonic Force** – two very influential early Hip Hop records . . . He also released the first UK female rap record 'Make Contact' by **Kute E.Q. And The Wow Wow Krew** on his **T-Mac** label in 1985, and put together and released the UK's first 12-inch compilation dance album *Remixture* in 1981.

CONTENTS

WHODUNNIT?

The chapter titles in this book all have one thing in common – they have all been titles of UK Top 20 singles. To test your knowledge see if you can name the artist(s) who scored the hit. Answers are on page 128.

ABBREVIATIONS

R&B = Rhythm & Blues
A&R = Artist & Repertoire
FM = Frequency Modulation
RIAA = Recording Industry Association of America
NARAS = National Academy of Recording Arts & Sciences
MOR = Middle Of The Road
S.A.W. = Stock Aitken & Waterman
Indie = Not associated with a major record label
Vaudeville = US equivalent of British Music Hall
Grammy = award given by NARAS
R'n'R = Rock 'n' Roll
F.A. = Football Association
FC = Football Club
Grand Ole Opry = The most famous US country music radio show
NKOTB = New Kids On The Block

YESTERDAY

THE EARLY DAYS OF RECORDS AND CHARTS

♦ In 1857 **Leon Scott** experimented with his **phonoautograph** which recorded on a cylinder, but it was **Thomas Edison** who patented his invention the **phonograph** (which played cylinders) just before the patent office closed on Christmas Eve, 1877. In the following month he started the world's first record label – the **Edison Speaking Phonograph Company** (which stayed in business until 1929). **Disc** recordings appeared in 1887 thanks to **Emile Berliner**, who also invented the **microphone**. The **Columbia Phonograph Company** was co-founded in 1887 by **Alexander Graham Bell** and its first stars, recorded on wax cylinders, were **John Philip Sousa's Band** and the **United States Marine Band**. The first recording by a popular solo artist was probably a short piano piece by 12-year-old **Josef Hoffman** in 1888. The first **commercial recordings** were manufactured for use in **phonograph parlours** on 25th May, 1889 and in the following year, on 5th Avenue in New York, the first **recording studio** opened.

♦ The **first listing** of the most popular records in the US (usually a Top 3) appeared in 1891 in *Phonogram* (a music industry magazine) and in *Phonoscope* which listed the month's top releases.

♦ The **first 'reasonably priced' home phonographs** ($40) appeared in 1894 which was the year that *Billboard* (the US music industry trade magazine) was first published and the year that **Columbia** became the leading company in the record business.

♦ In 1903 **Enrico Caruso** recorded 'Vesti La Giubba (On With The Motley)' which is claimed to be the world's first million-seller (a claim shared by **Len Spencer**'s 'Arkansas Traveler' and 'The Preacher And The Bear' by **Arthur Collins**). In 1908 the first double-sided discs appeared and five years later *Billboard* printed its first charts: 'Last Week's Ten Best-Sellers Among The Popular Songs' for sheet music, and 'Songs Heard In Vaudeville Last Week' for the most popular songs performed in Vaudeville. (Vaudeville is the US equivalent of music hall). In 1920 **Ben Selvin**'s 'Dardanella' became the first three-million seller and was heard on the new phenomenon, 'radio', which became immensely popular in the early 1920s. In 1925 the much recorded **Vernon Dalhart** released his famous 'The Prisoner's Song' which is reputed to have sold seven million copies. Amazingly, over 140 million records were sold in the US in 1927 – a figure which dropped dramatically to six million in 1932 when the Depression was at its height. In 1935 the first chart orientated radio show *Your Hit Parade* started in America, and **juke boxes** seemed to spring up everywhere.

♦ In the 1930s *Billboard* printed such charts as 'Popular Numbers Featured By Famous Singers And Leaders', 'Ten Best Records' And 'Songs With The Most Radio Plugs', and in July, 1940, they published their first official 'Best Selling Records' chart.

♦ In 1942 **Glenn Miller** was presented with the first gold record – it was for his million-selling 'Chattanooga Choo Choo'. Later that year, **Bing Crosby** recorded 'White Christmas' which went on to be the biggest-selling single of all time with sales of over 30 million worldwide.

♦ The first US album (simply a collection of 10-inch or 12-inch 78 rpm singles) chart was introduced in 1945. In 1948 **CBS** introduced the 33⅓rd rpm microgroove 'long playing' (LP) record while **RCA** brought out the first 45 rpm singles and record sales in the US broke the 250 million mark. The first million-selling LP was the **Original Cast** recording of *Oklahoma* in 1949. In Britain the first albums appeared in 1950 and the first 45 rpm singles in 1952, which was the year that a British record first topped the US chart, namely **Vera Lynn**'s 'Auf Wiedersehen Sweetheart' (in July). Four months later, the first British sales chart – a Top 12 –

No wonder **Bing Crosby** *is smiling – he had the best-selling single of all time under his belt.*

was introduced by *New Musical Express*.

CHART FIRSTS

♦ The first UK chart for record sales appeared in *New Musical Express* in November, 1952. It was headed by **Al Martino**'s 'Here In My Heart' (which had been a US chart-topper five months earlier). In America that week the no. 1 in *Billboard* was **Patti Page**'s 'I Went To Your Wedding'. Here's a selection of transatlantic no. 1 facts since that important date:

TYPE OF NO. 1	TITLE & ARTIST (UK AND US)	YEAR
FIRST MEDLEY	'LET'S HAVE ANOTHER PARTY' – WINIFRED ATWELL	1954
	'AQUARIUS' / 'LET THE SUNSHINE IN' – FIFTH DIMENSION	1969
FIRST POSTHUMOUS	'IT DOESN'T MATTER ANYMORE' – BUDDY HOLLY	1959
	'THE DOCK OF THE BAY' – OTIS REDDING	1968
FIRST DEATH DISC	'TELL LAURA I LOVE HER' – RICKY VALANCE	1960
	'TEEN ANGEL' – MARK DINNING	1960
FIRST TEENAGE ACT	'WHY DO FOOLS FALL IN LOVE' – FRANKIE LYMON & THE TEENAGERS (LEAD AGE 13)	1956
	'I SAW MOMMY KISSING SANTA CLAUS' – JIMMY BOYD (AGE 13)	1952
FIRST TEENAGE GIRL	'YOU DON'T KNOW' – HELEN SHAPIRO (AGE 14)	1961
	'I'M SORRY' – BRENDA LEE (AGE 15)	1960
FIRST COMIC/HUMORIST	'TEARS' – KEN DODD	1965
	'ST GEORGE & THE DRAGONET' – STAN FREBERG	1953
FIRST ONE HIT WONDER	'LITTLE THINGS MEAN A LOT' – KITTY KALLEN	1954
	'IT'S IN THE BOOK' – JOHNNY STANDLEY	1952
FIRST MIXED DUO	'COME OUTSIDE' – WENDY RICHARD & MIKE SARNE	1962
	'VAYA CON DIOS' – LES PAUL & MARY FORD	1953
FIRST ROCK INSTRUMENTAL	'HOOTS MON' – LORD ROCKINGHAM'S XI	1958
	'TEQUILA' – CHAMPS	1958
FIRST SONG TO TOP TWICE (By different acts)	'ANSWER ME' –DAVID WHITFIELD / FRANKIE LAINE (both 1953)	
	'GO AWAY LITTLE GIRL' – STEVE LAWRENCE (1963) DONNY OSMOND (1971)	
FIRST AFRICAN ACT	DANNY WILLIAMS – 'MOON RIVER'	1961
	HUGH MASAKELA – 'GRAZING IN THE GRASS'	1968
FIRST AUSTRALIAN FEMALE	'I SHOULD BE SO LUCKY' – KYLIE MINOGUE	1988
	'I AM WOMAN' – HELEN REDDY	1972
FIRST AUSTRALIAN MALE	'TWO LITTLE BOYS' – ROLF HARRIS	1969
	'I JUST WANT TO BE YOUR EVERYTHING' – ANDY GIBB	1977
FIRST AUSTRALIAN GROUP	'I'LL NEVER FIND ANOTHER YOU' – SEEKERS	1965
	'THE ONE THAT YOU LOVE' – AIR SUPPLY	1981
FIRST/ONLY AUSTRIAN ACT	'ROCK ME AMADEUS' – FALCO	1986
	'ROCK ME AMADEUS' – FALCO	1986
FIRST CANADIAN ACT	'DIANA' – PAUL ANKA	1957
	'SH-BOOM' – CREW CUTS	1954
FIRST DUTCH ACT	'MISSISSIPPI' – PUSSYCAT	1976
	'VENUS' – SHOCKING BLUE	1970
FIRST FRENCH ACT	'SHE' – CHARLES AZNAVOUR	1974
	'LOVE IS BLUE' – PAUL MAURIAT	1968
FIRST GERMAN ACT	'THE MODEL' / 'COMPUTER LOVE' – KRAFTWERK	1982
	'WONDERLAND BY NIGHT' – BERT KAEMPFERT	1961

TYPE OF NO. 1	TITLE & ARTIST (UK AND US)	YEAR
FIRST/ONLY GREEK ACT	'THE ROUSSOS PHENOMENON' E.P. – DEMIS ROUSSOS	1976
	'CHARIOTS OF FIRE' / 'TITLES' – VANGELIS	1982
FIRST IRISH FEMALE	'SOFTLY SOFTLY' – RUBY MURRAY	1955
	'NOTHING COMPARES 2 U' – SINEAD O'CONNOR	1990
FIRST ITALIAN ACT	'RIDE ON TIME' – BLACK BOX	1989
	'VOLARE' – DOMENICO MODUGNO	1958
FIRST/ONLY NORWEGIAN ACT	'THE SUN ALWAYS SHINES ON T.V.' – A-HA	1986
	'TAKE ON ME' – A-HA	1985

Oh Soulful Me-o! **Black Box** *were the first Italian act to top the British chart.*

TYPE OF NO. 1	TITLE & ARTIST (UK AND US)	YEAR
FIRST SCOTTISH FEMALE	'ONE DAY AT A TIME' – LENA MARTELL	1979
	'TO SIR WITH LOVE' – LULU	1967
FIRST SWEDISH ACT	'WATERLOO' – ABBA	1974
	'HOOKED ON A FEELING' – BLUE SWEDE	1974
FIRST WELSH FEMALE	'AS I LOVE YOU' – SHIRLEY BASSEY	1959
	'TOTAL ECLIPSE OF THE HEART' – BONNIE TYLER	1983

FIRST UK NO. 1s IN THE US

ACT	NO. 1 HIT	YEAR
FIRST UK VOCAL GROUP	'I WANT TO HOLD YOUR HAND' – BEATLES	1964
FIRST UK SOLOIST	'DOWNTOWN' – PETULA CLARK	1965
FIRST UK SOLO MALE	'SUNSHINE SUPERMAN' – DONOVAN	1966
FIRST BLACK SOLO MALE	'KUNG FU FIGHTING' – CARL DOUGLAS	1974
FIRST UK DUO	'A WORLD WITHOUT LOVE' – PETER & GORDON	1964
FIRST UK INSTRUMENTAL	'STRANGER ON THE SHORE' – MR. ACKER BILK	1962
FIRST UK INSTRUMENTAL GROUP	'TELSTAR' – TORNADOS	1962
FIRST UK SONG	'I SAW MOMMY KISSING SANTA CLAUS' – JIMMY BOYD (Composer TOMMIE CONNOR)	1952
FIRST UK FEMALE GROUP	'VENUS' – BANANARAMA	1986

VARIOUS NO. 1 FIRSTS IN THE UK

ACT	NO. 1 HIT	YEAR
FIRST UK ACT RECORDED IN US	'THE MINUTE YOU'RE GONE' – CLIFF RICHARD	1965
FIRST US FEMALE GROUP	'BABY LOVE' – SUPREMES	1964
FIRST BANNED SONG	'SUCH A NIGHT' – JOHNNIE RAY	1954
FIRST SKIFFLE RECORD	'GAMBLIN' MAN' – LONNIE DONEGAN	1957
FIRST CHOIR	'THERE'S NO ONE QUITE LIKE GRANDMA' – ST. WINIFRED'S SCHOOL CHOIR	1980
FIRST CHRISTMAS RECORD	'THE CHRISTMAS ALPHABET' – DICKIE VALENTINE	1955
FIRST BLACK ARTIST	'LET'S HAVE ANOTHER PARTY' – WINIFRED ATWELL	1954
FIRST BLACK SINGER	'MARY'S BOY CHILD' – HARRY BELAFONTE	1957
FIRST BLACK GROUP	'WHY DO FOOLS FALL IN LOVE' – TEENAGERS	1956
FIRST FEMALE DUO	'UPTOWN TOP RANKING' – ALTHIA & DONNA	1977
FIRST SPANISH ACT	'YES SIR I CAN BOOGIE' – BACCARA	1977
FIRST/ONLY ISRAELI ACT	'CINDERELLA ROCKAFELLA' – ESTHER & ABI OFARIM	1968
FIRST NO. 1 WITH NO FOLLOW-UP	'SUICIDE IS PAINLESS' – MASH	1980

VARIOUS US NO. 1 FIRSTS AND ONE-OFFS

FIRST SURF HIT	'SURF CITY' – JAN & DEAN	1963
FIRST BLACK MALE SOLO	'YOU SEND ME' – SAM COOKE	1957
FIRST BLACK FEMALE SOLO	'THE LOCO-MOTION' – LITTLE EVA	1962

TYPE OF NO. 1	TITLE & ARTIST (UK AND US)	YEAR
FIRST BLACK FEMALE GROUP	'WILL YOU LOVE ME TOMORROW' – SHIRELLES	1961
FIRST WHITE FEMALE GROUP	'MR. SANDMAN' – CHORDETTES	1954
ONLY INSTRUMENTAL DUO	'SLEEP WALK' – SANTO & JOHNNY	1959
ONLY CANADIAN FEMALE	'BLACK VELVET' – ALLANAH MYLES	1990
ONLY BELGIAN	'DOMINIQUE' – SINGING NUN (SOEUR SOURIRE)	1963
ONLY JAPANESE	'SUKIYAKI' – KYU SAKAMOTO	1963
ONLY CZECHOSLOVAKIAN	'MIAMI VICE THEME' – JAN HAMMER	1985

FIRST NO. 1s OF THE DECADES (50s–90s)

MALE SOLO SINGERS IN UK

AL MARTINO	'HERE IN MY HEART'	1952
MICHAEL HOLLIDAY	'STARRY EYED'	1960
LEE MARVIN	'WAND'RIN STAR'	1970
KENNY ROGERS	'COWARD OF THE COUNTY'	1980
ELTON JOHN	'SACRIFICE'	1990

MALE SOLO SINGERS IN THE US

JOHNNY STANDLEY	'IT'S IN THE BOOK'	1952
MARTY ROBBINS	'EL PASO'	1960
B.J. THOMAS	'RAINDROPS KEEP FALLIN' ON MY HEAD'	1970
MICHAEL JACKSON	'ROCK WITH YOU'	1980
PHIL COLLINS	'ANOTHER DAY IN PARADISE'	1990

FEMALE SOLO SINGERS IN THE UK

JO STAFFORD	'YOU BELONG TO ME'	1953
PETULA CLARK	'SAILOR'	1961
DANA	'ALL KINDS OF EVERYTHING'	1970
FERN KINNEY	'TOGETHER WE ARE BEAUTIFUL'	1980
KYLIE MINOGUE	'TEARS ON MY PILLOW'	1990

FEMALE SOLO SINGERS IN THE US

PATTI PAGE	'I WENT TO YOUR WEDDING'	1952
CONNIE FRANCIS	'EVERYBODY'S SOMEBODY'S FOOL'	1960
DIANA ROSS	'AIN'T NO MOUNTAIN HIGH ENOUGH'	1970
OLIVIA NEWTON-JOHN	'MAGIC'	1980
PAULA ABDUL	'OPPOSITES ATTRACT'	1990

VOCAL GROUPS/DUOS IN THE UK

STARGAZERS	'BROKEN WINGS'	1953
EVERLY BROTHERS	'CATHY'S CLOWN'	1960
EDISON LIGHTHOUSE	'LOVE GROWS (WHERE MY ROSEMARY GOES)'	1970
PRETENDERS	'BRASS IN POCKET'	1980
BAND AID II	'DO THEY KNOW IT'S CHRISTMAS'	1990

VOCAL GROUPS/DUOS IN THE US

MILLS BROTHERS	'THE GLOW WORM'	1952
EVERLY BROTHERS	'CATHY'S CLOWN'	1960
JACKSON 5	'I WANT YOU BACK'	1970
CAPTAIN & TENNILLE	'DO THAT TO ME ONE MORE TIME'	1980
WILSON PHILLIPS	'HOLD ON'	1990

TYPE OF NO. 1	TITLE & ARTIST (UK AND US)	YEAR
INTRUMENTALISTS IN THE UK		
MANTOVANI	'MOULIN ROUGE'	1953
SHADOWS	'APACHE'	1960
ROYAL SCOTS DRAGOON GUARDS	'AMAZING GRACE'	1972
KRAFTWERK	'THE MODEL' / 'COMPUTER LOVE'	1982
INSTRUMENTALISTS IN THE US		
PERCY FAITH	SONG FROM 'MOULIN ROUGE'	1953
PERCY FAITH	THEME FROM 'A SUMMER PLACE'	1960
ISAAC HAYES	THEME FROM 'SHAFT'	1971
VANGELIS	'CHARIOTS OF FIRE' / 'TITLES'	1982

MORE FIRSTS

♦ The first **radio commercial** was broadcast on the New York station WEAS on 28th August, 1922. It was an advertisement for an estate agent and it lasted ten minutes.

♦ The first **commercial radio station** in the UK was LBC, the London based news-orientated station, which was launched on 8th October, 1976.

♦ The first demonstration of **FM (frequency modulation) radio** took place on 5th January, 1940 in the US and the first show, which was called *On The Air* was broadcast a year later.

♦ The first **Mersey Beat magazine** came out on 6th July, 1961 and included a piece by John Lennon on the dubious origins of The Beatles.

♦ The first **punk magazine**, *Sniffin' Glue*, was launched in August, 1975 by Mark Perry who later led the punk group Alternative TV.

♦ **Bob Dylan's first recording** was his appearance on Harry Belafonte's album *Midnight Special* recorded on 24th April, 1961. Early in 1962 a reviewer in the US music trade magazine *Billboard* said that: 'He could have a big following when he finds a style of his own'.

♦ **Little Richard's first recording** was on 16th October, 1951. His first release was 'Taxi Blues'.

♦ **Lonnie Donegan** was the **first artist to get an EP on the**

Skiffle king **Lonnie Donegan.**

UK charts when his 'Skiffle Session' EP made the Top 20 in 1956. In the same year **Frank Sinatra**'s *Songs For Swinging Lovers* became the **first album** to accomplish a similar feat.

♦ The first **no. 1 hit on which the performer wrote/sang/ arranged/produced and played all the instruments** was 'A Different Corner' by **George Michael**, in 1986.

♦ The first **die cut single** is claimed to be **Bobby Caldwell**'s heart-shaped disc 'What You Won't Do For Love'. There were 50 000 copies pressed on red plastic in the US for Valentine's day in 1979. They each sold for

$7.98 (£5) which was far above the normal single price, so it certainly did show what the record buyers would do for love!

♦ **Britain's first cassette-only single** was 'C30, C60, C90, Go' by **Bow Wow Wow** in 1980. The act, which once included Lieutenant Lush (later known as Boy George), grabbed a great deal of media attention thanks in part to their photogenic 15-year-old singer Annabella Lwin and their manager Malcolm McLaren – who at one time was accused by Annabella's mother of kidnapping her!

♦ The first **12-inch single released in the UK** is claimed to be **Undisputed Truth**'s 'You & Me = Love' which came out in January, 1977.

♦ The first **video single** is said to be **Human League**'s 1983 release 'Love Action' which included their hits 'Don't You Want Me' and 'Mirror Man' – it sold for £11.99 ($19).

♦ The first **UK video jukebox chart** appeared on 21st May, 1984, and the top record was 'I Want To Break Free' which featured **Queen** in drag.

♦ The first **week that every record in the UK Top 75 was available as a 12-inch single** was 28th September, 1985.

♦ The first **3D picture disc** was 'I Love You' by **Yello**, released in 1983. It came complete with the 3D glasses.

♦ The first **video-only single** was **Sigue Sigue Sputnik**'s 'Sex Bom Boogie' released in 1986. It was filmed at the Royal Albert Hall in London and retailed for £4.99 ($8).

♦ The credit for producing the **first hologram sleeve** is claimed by the album of *Time*, the musical

Morrisey, *the last of the famous international playboys, had a first week triple chart-topper.*

staged by Dave Clark, in 1986.

♦ The first **simultaneous album and video release** was *Word Of Mouth* by **Toni Basil** on the Radialchoice label in April, 1981. The album charted in the UK a year later thanks to her huge international hit 'Mickey'.

♦ The first **video to sell a million copies in the UK** alone was *Dirty Dancing*, in 1991.

♦ There are many claims for the **most expensive video** ever but surely the most costly video resulting in a 'flop' was the $600 000 **Kenny Rogers** video for *Planet Texas* (1989) which was not a hit in either the pop or country charts.

♦ Neither **The Smiths** nor their leader **Morrissey** have ever topped the singles chart, but Morrissey became the **first act to enter Britain's Cassette, 12-inch and CD singles charts in the top spot**. He achieved this with 'Last Of The Famous International Playboys' in 1989.

♦ The first **singles not available on 7-inch vinyl to enter the US Top 100** were **De La Soul**'s 'Me Myself And I' and **Whistle**'s 'Right Next To Me' – both came in on 3rd June, 1989. The first one on a *major* label was **Billy Squier's** 'Don't Say You Love Me' three weeks later.

♦ In August, 1989, RCA became the **first major label to stop sending 7-inch singles to US radio stations**. A&M and IRS had already changed to CD and cassette-only. The **first company to phase out 7-inch vinyl altogether in the US** was WEA in January 1990. In April, 1990, a survey showed that 42 of the US Top 100 were not available on 7-inch singles.

♦ The **shortest album** is by **Gadfly** whose 6-song instrumental recording lasts a total of 32 seconds! The artist told *Record Mirror*'s Alan Jones 'It would have been shorter but I got carried away with the solo!'

♦ For the record – the first **demonstration of the CD** was in Europe in April, 1981, and this new format was officially launched in the UK in March, 1983.

♦ The first **five albums to sell a million on cassette in the UK** were: **Dire Straits**' *Brothers In Arms*, **Michael Jackson**'s *Thriller* and *Bad*, **Kylie Minogue**'s *Kylie* and **Jason Donovan**'s *Ten Good Reasons*.

♦ The first **million selling CDs** were: the **Soundtrack** to *Dirty Dancing*, **Def Leppard**'s *Hysteria* and **George Michael**'s *Faith*. Incidentally, *Dirty Dancing* set another record when Volume 2 of the movie soundtrack hit no. 3 on the US charts at the same time that Volume 1 held the top position.

♦ A UK survey from June, 1989, showed that for the first **time more money was earned by the sale of CD albums** than by their vinyl equivalents.

♦ The first **album only available on cassette or CD** to chart in the US was *Touch Me Tonight – The Best of Shooting Star* on 4th November, 1989.

♦ The American CD Album Chart was dropped by *Billboard* on 31st March, 1990 – proof that this new medium had come of age and was accepted by record buyers across the nation.

♦ The **most expensive CD set** was *The Complete Mozart Edition* – a 180 CD, 200-hour set that was released by Phillips in 1990, costing £1400 ($2250).

Sheffield's finest metal band **Def Leppard** *were the first group to sell a million copies of a CD.*

THE WINNER TAKES IT ALL

GRAMMY AWARDS

♦ The most prestigious music award in the US is the **Grammy** which has been presented by the National Academy of Recording Arts and Sciences (NARAS) since 1958. Their selections for **Top Single** and **Top New Artist** each year were as follows:

TOP SINGLE	ARTIST
1958 'VOLARE'	DOMENICO MODUGNO
1959 'MACK THE KNIFE'	BOBBY DARIN
1960 'THEME FROM "A SUMMER PLACE"'	PERCY FAITH
1961 'MOON RIVER'	HENRY MANCINI
1962 'I LEFT MY HEART IN SAN FRANCISCO'	TONY BENNETT
1963 'DAYS OF WINE AND ROSES'	HENRY MANCINI
1964 'THE GIRL FROM IPANEMA'	STAN GETZ & ASTRUD GILBERTO
1965 'A TASTE OF HONEY'	HERB ALPERT
1966 'STRANGERS IN THE NIGHT'	FRANK SINATRA
1967 'UP-UP AND AWAY'	5TH DIMENSION
1968 'MRS. ROBINSON'	SIMON & GARFUNKEL
1969 'AQUARIUS' / 'LET THE SUNSHINE IN'	5TH DIMENSION
1970 'BRIDGE OVER TROUBLED WATERS'	SIMON & GARFUNKEL
1971 'IT'S TOO LATE'	CAROLE KING
1972 'THE FIRST TIME EVER I SAW YOUR FACE'	ROBERTA FLACK
1973 'KILLING ME SOFTLY WITH HIS SONG'	ROBERTA FLACK
1974 'I HONESTLY LOVE YOU'	OLIVIA NEWTON-JOHN
1975 'LOVE WILL KEEP US TOGETHER'	CAPTAIN & TENNILLE
1976 'THIS MASQUERADE'	GEORGE BENSON
1977 'HOTEL CALIFORNIA'	EAGLES
1978 'JUST THE WAY YOU ARE'	BILLY JOEL
1979 'WHAT A FOOL BELIEVES'	DOOBIE BROTHERS
1980 'SAILING'	CHRISTOPHER CROSS
1981 'BETTE DAVIS EYES'	KIM CARNES
1982 'ROSANNA'	TOTO
1983 'BEAT IT'	MICHAEL JACKSON
1984 'WHAT'S LOVE GOT TO DO WITH IT'	TINA TURNER
1985 'WE ARE THE WORLD'	USA FOR AFRICA
1986 'HIGHER LOVE'	STEVE WINWOOD
1987 'GRACELAND'	PAUL SIMON
1988 'DON'T WORRY, BE HAPPY'	BOBBY McFERRIN

1989	'WIND BENEATH MY WINGS'	BETTE MIDLER
1990	'ANOTHER DAY IN PARADISE'	PHIL COLLINS

BEST NEW ACT

1959	BOBBY DARIN
1960	BOB NEWHART
1961	PETER NERO
1962	ROBERT GOULET
1963	SWINGLE SINGERS
1964	BEATLES
1965	TOM JONES
1966	No Award made
1967	BOBBIE GENTRY
1968	JOSE FELICIANO
1969	CROSBY, STILLS & NASH
1970	CARPENTERS
1971	CARLY SIMON
1972	AMERICA
1973	BETTE MIDLER
1974	MARVIN HAMLISCH
1975	NATALIE COLE
1976	STARLAND VOCAL BAND
1977	DEBBY BOONE
1978	A TASTE OF HONEY

Sixteen years after winning the Grammy for Best New Artist the divine **Bette Midler** *won the Grammy Record of the Year award.*

Girl you know it's true that **Milli Vanilli**, *those great pretenders, are the only act to return their Grammy award.*

1979 RICKIE LEE JONES
1980 CHRISTOPHER CROSS
1981 SHEENA EASTON
1982 MEN AT WORK
1983 CULTURE CLUB
1984 CYNDI LAUPER
1985 SADE
1986 BRUCE HORNSBY & THE RANGE
1987 JODY WATLEY
1988 TRACY CHAPMAN
1989 MILLI VANILLI (Award returned)
1990 MARIAH CAREY

♦ The only act to return a
Grammy was **Milli Vanilli**
(1989) after it was announced that
they did not sing on their hits.

The person with the most
nominations for the prestigious
Grammy awards is producer/
arranger/composer and performer
Quincy Jones who has had 74 to
date. The runner-up is orchestra
leader/arranger/composer **Henry
Mancini** who has had 71.

THE ROCK 'N' ROLL
HALL OF FAME

♦ The Rock 'n' Roll Hall of Fame
was started in 1986 with the aim
of honouring those who have
helped to make rock music the
institution it is today. The
chairman of the project is Atlantic
Records boss Ahmet Ertegun and
many record companies and major
artists have helped to raise the
$50 million needed to build the
Hall. It will be based in a complex
in Cleveland, Ohio (the city where
the original rock 'n' roll D.J. Alan
Freed began his career) and will
house rock memorabilia from the
last 40 years. It is hoped that it
will be open to the public by the
mid-90s.

♦ To date, the performers who
have been inducted to the
prestigious body of the Rock 'n'
Roll Hall of Fame are:

HANK BALLARD
LAVERN BAKER
BEACH BOYS
BEATLES
CHUCK BERRY
JAMES BROWN
BYRDS
RAY CHARLES
COASTERS
EDDIE COCHRAN
SAM COOKE
BOBBY DARIN
BO DIDDLEY
DION
FATS DOMINO
DRIFTERS
BOB DYLAN
EVERLY BROTHERS
FOUR SEASONS
FOUR TOPS
ARETHA FRANKLIN
MARVIN GAYE
BILL HALEY
BUDDY HOLLY
JOHN LEE HOOKER
IMPRESSIONS
B.B. KING
KINKS
JERRY LEE LEWIS
LITTLE RICHARD
CLYDE MCPHATTER
RICKY NELSON
ROY ORBISON
CARL PERKINS
WILSON PICKETT
PLATTERS
ELVIS PRESLEY
OTIS REDDING
JIMMY REED
SMOKEY ROBINSON
ROLLING STONES
SIMON & GARFUNKEL
SUPREMES
TEMPTATIONS
BIG JOE TURNER
IKE & TINA TURNER
MUDDY WATERS
WHO
JACKIE WILSON
STEVIE WONDER

BRITS AWARDS

♦ The British equivalent of the Grammy Awards are the **BRITS** awards given by the British Phonographic Industry (B.P.I.) and since their introduction winners have included:

BEST BRITISH SINGLE

1981 'TAINTED LOVE' – SOFT CELL
1982 'COME ON EILEEN' – DEXY'S MIDNIGHT RUNNERS
1983 'KARMA CHAMELEON' – CULTURE CLUB
1984 'RELAX' – FRANKIE GOES TO HOLLYWOOD
1985 'EVERYBODY WANTS TO RULE THE WORLD' – TEARS FOR FEARS
1986 'WEST END GIRLS' – PET SHOP BOYS
1987 'NEVER GONNA GIVE YOU UP' – RICK ASTLEY
1988 'PERFECT' – FAIRGROUND ATTRACTION
1989 'ANOTHER DAY IN PARADISE' – PHIL COLLINS
1990 'ENJOY THE SILENCE' – DEPECHE MODE

BEST BRITISH NEWCOMER

1981 HUMAN LEAGUE
1982 YAZOO
1983 PAUL YOUNG
1984 FRANKIE GOES TO HOLLYWOOD
1985 GO WEST
1986 HOUSEMARTINS
1987 WET WET WET
1988 BROS
1989 LISA STANSFIELD
1990 BETTY BOO

♦ The first act to return a **BRITS** award was **Fine Young Cannibals**, in 1990. The reason for this action was that the group felt that the show (which was produced by one time Tory candidate and hit-maker **Jonathan King**) was a promotion for the Tory party, featuring as it did Mrs. Thatcher, speaking about her favourite records – which, incidentally, included 'Telstar' by the **Tornados** and 'How Much is That Doggie in The Window' (a very capitalist enquiry).

EUROVISION

♦ For 35 years the **Eurovision Song Contest** has been the major song competition in Europe, and

Lisa Stansfield, *voted Britain's best new singer of 1989, is now known all around the world.*

over those years it has produced many big hits, not only in the countries that take part but all around the world. It has introduced us to acts like **Abba**, **Bucks Fizz**, **Dana**, **Black Lace**, and **Celine Dion** – and perhaps helped to precipitate the end of the chart careers of acts such as **Kathy Kirby**, **Ronnie Carroll**, **Lulu**, **Mary Hopkin**, **Clodagh Rodgers** and **Lynsey De Paul**!

The winners to date:

YEAR	TITLE	SINGER (COUNTRY)	UK CHART POSITION
1956	'REFRAINS'	LYS ASSIA (SWITZERLAND)	–
1957	'NET ALSTOWN'	CORRY BROKKEN (NETHERLANDS)	–
1958	'DORS MON AMOUR'	ANDRE CLAVEON (FRANCE)	–
1959	'EENE BEETJE'	TEDDY SCHOLTEN (NETHERLANDS)	–
1960	'TOM PILLIBI'	JACQUELINE BOYER (FRANCE)	33
1961	'NOUS, LES AMOUREUX'	JEAN CLAUDE PASCAL (LUXEMBOURG)	–
1962	'UN PREMIER AMOUR'	ISABELLE AUBRET (FRANCE)	–
1963	'DANSEVISE'	GRETHE & JORGEN INGMAN (DENMARK)	–
1964	'NON HO L'ETA PER AMARTI'	GIGLIOLA CINQUETTI (ITALY)	17
1965	'POUPEE DE CIRE POUPEE DE SON'	FRANCE GALL (LUXEMBOURG)	–
1966	'MERCI CHERIE'	UDO JERGENS (AUSTRIA)	–
1967	'PUPPET ON A STRING'	SANDIE SHAW (UK)	1
1968	'LA LA LA'	MASSIEL (SPAIN)	35
1969	'UN JOUR, UN ENFANT'*	FRIDA BOCCANA (FRANCE)	–
1969	'DE TROUBADOR'*	LENNIE KUHR (HOLLAND)	–
1969	'BOOM BANG A BANG'*	LULU (UK)	2
1969	'UNO CANTANDO'*	SALOME (SPAIN)	–
1970	'ALL KINDS OF EVERYTHING'	DANA (EIRE)	1
1971	'UN BANC, UN ARBRE, UNE RUE'	SEVERIN (MONACO)	9
1972	'APRES TOIS' (COME WHAT MAY)	VICKY LEANDROS (LUXEMBOURG)	2
1973	'TU TE RECONNAITRAS (WONDERFUL DREAM)	ANNE MARIE DAVID (LUXEMBOURG)	13
1974	'WATERLOO'	ABBA (SWEDEN)	1
1975	'DING A DONG'	TEACH IN (HOLLAND)	13
1976	'SAVE YOUR KISSES FOR ME'	BROTHERHOOD OF MAN (UK)	1
1977	'L'OISEAU ET L'ENFANT'	MARIE MYRIAM (FRANCE)	42
1978	'A BA NI BI'	IZHAR COHEN & ALPHABETA (ISRAEL)	20
1979	'HALLELUJAH'	MILK & HONEY (ISRAEL)	5
1980	'WHAT'S ANOTHER YEAR'	JOHNNY LOGAN (EIRE)	1
1981	'MAKING YOUR MIND UP'	BUCKS FIZZ (UK)	1
1982	'A LITTLE PEACE'	NICOLE (W. GERMANY)	1
1983	'SI LA VIE EST CADEAU'	CORINNINE HERMES (LUXEMBOURG)	–
1984	'DIGGY LOO DIGGEY LEY'	HERREYS (SWEDEN)	46
1985	'LA DET SWINGE' (LET IT SWING)	BOBBY SOCKS (NORWAY)	44
1986	'J'AIME LA VIE'	SANDRA KIM (BELGIUM)	–
1987	'HOLD ME NOW'	JOHNNY LOGAN (EIRE)	2
1988	'NE PARTEZ PAS SANS MOI'	CELINE DION (SWITZERLAND)	–
1989	'ROCK ME'	RIVA (YUGOSLAVIA)	–
1990	'INSIEME 1992' (ALL TOGETHER 1992)	TOTO CUTUGNO (ITALY)	–
1991	'FANGAD AV EN STORMVIND'	CAROLA (SWEDEN)	–

* = JOINT WINNERS

Other British entries:

YEAR	TITLE	SINGER	UK CHART	EUROVISION POSITION
1957	'ALL'	PATRICIA BREDEN	–	6
1959	'SING LITTLE BIRDIE'	PEARL CARR & TEDDY JOHNSON	12	2
1960	'LOOKING HIGH HIGH HIGH'	BRYAN JOHNSON	20	2
1961	'ARE YOU SURE'	ALLISONS	2	2
1962	'RING A DING GIRL'	RONNIE CARROLL	46	4
1963	'SAY WONDERFUL THINGS'	RONNIE CARROLL	6	4
1964	'I LOVE THE LITTLE THINGS'	MATT MONRO	–	2
1965	'I BELONG'	KATHY KIRBY	36	2
1966	'A MAN WITHOUT LOVE'	KENNETH MCKELLAR	30	7
1968	'CONGRATULATIONS'	CLIFF RICHARD	1	2
1970	'KNOCK, KNOCK, WHO'S THERE?'	MARY HOPKIN	2	2
1971	'JACK IN THE BOX'	CLODAGH RODGERS	4	4
1972	'BEG, STEAL OR BORROW'	NEW SEEKERS	2	2
1973	'POWER TO ALL OUR FRIENDS'	CLIFF RICHARD	4	4
1974	'LONG LIVE LOVE'	OLIVIA NEWTON-JOHN	11	4
1975	'LET ME BE THE ONE'	SHADOWS	12	2
1977	'ROCK BOTTOM'	LYNSEY DE PAUL & MIKE MORAN	19	2
1978	'BAD OLD DAYS'	COCO	13	11
1979	'MARY ANNE'	BLACK LACE	42	7
1980	'LOVE ENOUGH FOR TWO'	PRIMA DONNA	48	3
1982	'ONE STEP FURTHER'	BARDO	2	7
1983	'I'M NEVER GIVING UP'	SWEET DREAMS	21	6
1984	'LOVE GAMES'	BELLE & THE DEVOTIONS	11	7
1985	'LOVE IS'	VIKKI WATSON	49	5
1986	'RUNNER IN THE NIGHT'	RYDER	96	7
1987	'ONLY THE LIGHT'	RIKKI	98	13
1988	'GO'	SCOTT FITZGERALD	52	2
1989	'WHY DO I ALWAYS GET IT WRONG?'	LIVE REPORT	73	2
1990	'GIVE A LITTLE LOVE BACK TO THE WORLD'	EMMA	33	6
1991	'A MESSAGE TO YOUR HEART'	SAMANTHA JANUS	30	10

♦ The only Eurovision winner to hit the US Top 20 was **Abba**'s 'Waterloo' (no. 6). **Brotherhood of Man**'s 'Save Your Kisses For Me', which made it to no. 27, was the only other American Top 40 entry.

♦ Interestingly though, less successful Eurovision songs like 'Love Is Blue' by **Paul Mauriat** and 'Eres Tu' by **Mocedades** were big hits in the USA (no. 1 in 1968 and no. 9 in 1974, respectively). It's also worth mentioning that Sweden's 1982 entry, **Force**, hit in both the US and UK in 1986 when they changed their name to **Europe**. Also, French-Canadian **Celine Dion**, who first hit the US Top 10 in 1991, won the contest for Switzerland in 1988.

GOLD

GOING FOR GOLD

♦ In the US in 1958, the **Record Industry Association of America** (RIAA) started certifying **gold singles** and **albums**.

♦ For singles, a million sales justified a gold disc until 1989 when the magic total was halved. Half a million sales of an LP is awarded with a gold disc. They introduced **platinum singles** and **albums** (for million-sellers) in 1976 and **multi-platinum album awards** in 1985. This does not mean that records before those dates did not sell enough copies to qualify, and it should be remembered that some companies (most notably **Motown**) did not belong to the RIAA in the early days, which means that many records, especially singles, that passed the million mark did not get official gold records. Here are some interesting facts about RIAA certified gold and platinum records in the US:

♦ The first certified gold singles were **Elvis Presley**'s 'Don't' and **Perry Como**'s 'Catch A Falling Star' which were both on RCA, the first company to comply with RIAA's certification requirements.

♦ Pop/folk threesome the **Kingston Trio** were both the first group to earn a certified gold single and the first to earn a gold record for a live album. The records concerned were 'Tom Dooley' in 1958, and *From The Hungry I* in 1959.

♦ The first platinum single was 'Disco Lady' by **Johnnie Taylor** and the first earned by a group was 'Kiss And Say Goodbye' by the **Manhattans** – the two soul smashes were hits in 1976, the year the platinum single was introduced.

♦ The biggest-selling debut album by a group was **Boston**'s eponymous album in 1976 which has sold over ten million. The top-selling debut album by a male artist is *Faith* by **George Michael** with sales of more than seven million.

♦ The country performer with the most gold albums is **Willie Nelson**, who has earned 17 since 1975.

♦ The first certified gold album was the soundtrack album of *Oklahoma* released in 1955, and the first earned by a solo artist was **Tennessee Ernie Ford**'s *Hymns* which came out in in 1956. The first certified platinum record was *The Eagles' Greatest Hits* in February 1976.

♦ The female artist with the most gold albums is **Barbra Streisand** with 34 and the female singer with the most gold singles is **Aretha Franklin** with 14 – collected between 1967–73.

♦ **Elton John** has earned more gold albums worldwide than any other British solo artist. He received his first in 1970 and has picked up another 23 since then.

♦ **Chicago**, who picked up their first gold album in 1972, have earned 14 platinum records – a total no other group has yet matched.

♦ The biggest-selling *Greatest Hits* albums is by the **Eagles**, which has passed the 12 million mark.

♦ **Peter Frampton**'s *Frampton Comes Alive!* album is not only the biggest selling live LP of all time, with sales of over six million, but also the biggest selling double album by a solo artist.

♦ The only artist to date to notch up three consecutive platinum

Bing Crosby's *platinum disc for the sales of 'Silent Night' – the kind of award every artist dreams about.*

double albums is **Donna Summer** – they were: *Live And More* in 1978, *Bad Girls* in 1979 and *On The Radio/Greatest Hits Vols 1 & 2* in 1980.

♦ The only time three successive UK no. 1 singles sold a million copies in the UK alone occurred in September, 1989 when 'Two Tribes' by **Frankie Goes To Hollywood** was followed to the top by **George Michael**'s 'Careless Whisper' and then by **Stevie Wonder**'s 'I Just Called To Say I Love You'. With the current decline in the sales of singles this is a feat that is most unlikely to happen ever again.

♦ Whilst on this subject it's worth mentioning that **Frankie Goes To Hollywood** (see above) were the first act to sell over a million in the UK alone on their first two releases – 'Relax' (which also earned them a US gold disc) and 'Two Tribes'.

♦ Britain's best-selling single ever is **Band Aid**'s 'Do They Know It's Christmas' which has sold over 3.5 million since its release in 1984. The least time a no. 1 record has spent on the UK Top 75 is just six weeks (three of those at no. 1) – a record set up by **Band Aid II** with 'Do They Know It's Christmas' in 1990.

♦ Which British act received five gold albums in 1961 when arriving in America for a tour? It was orchestra leader **Mantovani**. They were for his LPs *Strauss Waltzes, Christmas Carols, Song Hits From Theatreland, Film Encores* and *Gems Forever* – all US Top 10 hits in the 50s.

♦ When **Cher** was presented with a gold disc for her LP *Take Me Home* in 1979, it had only sold 700 000. Her record company

*Over seven million Americans had faith in **George Michael**'s debut solo album.*

Polygram then pressed another 300 000 to make up the requirement, but they did not sell. However, she was allowed to keep the disc.

♦ The only album to sell over one million copies in the UK in 1982 was by a group of Americans who only managed to get the album to no. 146 in their homeland. They were **The Kids From Fame** with their eponymous LP.

♦ The first record to be requested one million times from **Personics**, the US company who legally make up albums of any tracks on request, was **Ben E.**

Ben E. King's *28-year-old single made him the people's choice in the US.*

King's 'Stand By Me' in August, 1989.

♦ After the gold standard for singles sales in the US was dropped from one million sales to half a million in 1989, due to the decline in singles sales, the first 'new' gold discs were awarded as follows:

BOBBY McFERRIN – 'DON'T WORRY
  BE HAPPY'
ESCAPE CLUB – 'WILD WILD WEST'
PHIL COLLINS – 'GROOVY KIND OF
  LOVE'
BEACH BOYS – 'KOKOMO' (which
  subsequently sold over a million and
  earned a 'new' platinum single)

MILLION-SELLERS

♦ For a single to sell over a million copies is a big achievement and, as you might expect, it usually only happens to a record that makes the top end of the charts. However, there are exceptions to this rule as you will see from the list (opposite) of US singles that passed that magic sales figure without making the Top 20. Nearly all of them are R&B (i.e. rhythm and blues), country or dance music records where sales popularity was not reflected in the mainstream airplay reports which constitute much of the US Top 100 data.

ARTIST	TITLE	PEAK POSITION	YEAR
JOHN ANDERSON	SWINGIN'	43	1983
AFRIKA BAMBAATAA	PLANET ROCK	48	1982
ROB BASE & D.J. E–Z ROCK	IT TAKES TWO	36	1989
KURTIS BLOW	THE BREAKS	87	1980
CHUCK BROWN	BUSTIN' LOOSE	34	1979
JAMES BROWN	THE PAYBACK	34	1974
JERRY BUTLER/BRENDA LEE EAGER	AIN'T UNDERSTANDING MELLOW	21	1972
C-COMPANY	BATTLE HYMN OF LT. CALLEY	37	1971
CARL CARLTON	SHE'S A BAD MAMA JAMA	22	1981
CHICAGO BEARS SHUFFLIN' CREW	SUPERBOWL SHUFFLE	41	1986
JIMMY DEAN	I.O.U.	35	1976
DOUG E. FRESH & GET FRESH CREW	THE SHOW	–	1986
FUNKADELIC	ONE NATION UNDER A GROOVE	28	1978
DAN HARTMAN	INSTANT REPLAY	29	1979
INDEPENDENTS	LEAVING ME	21	1973
WAYLON JENNINGS	THEME FROM 'THE DUKES OF HAZZARD'	21	1980
JONES GIRLS	YOU'RE GONNA MAKE ME LOVE SOMEBODY ELSE	38	1979
EVELYN 'CHAMPAGNE' KING	I DON'T KNOW IF IT'S RIGHT	23	1979
JACKIE MOORE	PRECIOUS, PRECIOUS	30	1971
MTUME	JUICY FRUIT	45	1983
TEDDY PENDERGRASS	CLOSE THE DOOR	25	1978
ELVIS PRESLEY	MY WAY	22	1977
CHARLEY PRIDE	KISS AN ANGEL GOOD MORNING	21	1972
SALT-N-PEPA	EXPRESSION	26	1990
FRANKIE SMITH	DOUBLE DUTCH BUS	30	1981
RED SOVINE	TEDDY BEAR	40	1976
VILLAGE PEOPLE	MACHO MAN	25	1978
FRED WESLEY & THE JB'S	DOIN' IT TO DEATH	22	1973
BOBBY WOMACK	HARRY HIPPIE	31	1972

♦ Apart from pop singles, **children's records**, which are never included in chart calculations, have also reached the million mark. As you might expect, the most successful record company in this market is **Disney** who saw 30 of their singles go gold in the 80s, with three of them ('Bambi', '101 Dalmatians' and 'Star Wars') selling over two million copies each.

♦ It is not so unusual for an album to go gold (500 000 sales) without hitting the Top 20 but it's rare for one to have sales of that quantity without making the US Top 200 chart at all. The following are exceptions to this rule:

ARTIST	TITLE	YEAR WENT GOLD
POP RECORDINGS		
DR. MARK BESHARA	*ASTRAL SOUNDS/A NATURAL HIGH*	1982
CANDLE	*THE MUSIC MACHINE*	1981
CANDLE	*BULLFROGS & BUTTERFLIES*	1984
DORIS DAY	*GREATEST HITS*	1968
BOB DYLAN	*BOB DYLAN*	1973
EVERLY BROTHERS	*THE VERY BEST OF . . .*	1986
EVIE	*COME ON RING THOSE BELLS*	1987
PERCY FAITH	*VIVA - THE MUSIC OF MEXICO*	1963
DAN FOGELBERG	*HOME FREE*	1979
RAY LYNCH	*DEEP BREAKFAST*	1989
GLENN MILLER	*GLENN MILLER STORY*	1968
GLENN MILLER	*A MEMORIAL 1944-1969*	1986
GLENN MILLER	*PURE GOLD*	1984
ELVIS PRESLEY	*PURE GOLD*	1977
REO SPEEDWAGON	*R.E.O./T.W.O.*	1981
SOUNDTRACK	*VICTORY AT SEA*	1964
STYX	*BEST OF . . .*	1984
BILLY VAUGHAN	*THE GOLDEN INSTRUMENTALS*	1969
VIOLENT FEMMES	*VIOLENT FEMMES*	1987
CLASSICAL RECORDINGS		
MAURICE ANDRE/		
PAILLARD CHAMBER ORCH.	*THE PACHELBEL CANON*	1985
LEONARD BERNSTEIN	*GERSHWIN: AN AMERICAN IN PARIS*	1986
ANDRE KOSTELANETZ	*WONDERLAND OF GOLDEN HITS*	1965
EUGENE ORMANDY	*HANDEL: MESSIAH*	1963
HERBERT VON KARAJAN	*BETHOVEN: THE NINE SYMPHONIES*	1977
COUNTRY RECORDINGS		
BELLAMY BROTHERS	*GREATEST HITS*	1986
PATSY CLINE	*GREATEST HITS*	1985
DAVID ALLAN COE	*GREATEST HITS*	1983
EARL THOMAS CONLEY	*GREATEST HITS*	1989
LEE GREENWOOD	*INSIDE OUT*	1986
MERLE HAGGARD	*THE BEST OF . . .*	1972
MERLE HAGGARD	*HIS EPIC HITS*	1989
KENDALLS	*HEAVEN'S JUST A SIN AWAY*	1982
LORETTA LYNN	*GREATEST HITS*	1972
LORETTA LYNN	*GREATEST HITS VOL. 2*	1981
REBA McENTIRE	*WHOEVER'S IN NEW ENGLAND*	1987
REBA McENTIRE	*WHAT AM I GONNA DO ABOUT YOU*	1987
RONNIE MILSAP	*LIVE*	1979
OAK RIDGE BOYS	*HAVE ARRIVED*	1980
DOLLY PARTON	*BEST OF . . .*	1978
CHARLEY PRIDE	*COUNTRY*	1975
MARTY ROBBINS	*ALL TIME GREATEST HITS*	1982
RICKY SKAGGS	*DON'T CHEAT IN OUR HOMETOWN*	1984
RAY STEVENS	*I HAVE RETURNED*	1989
GEORGE STRAIT	*STRAIT COUNTRY*	1988
GEORGE STRAIT	*STRAIT FROM THE HEART*	1987

ARTIST	TITLE	YEAR WENT GOLD
GEORGE STRAIT	*SOMETHING SPECIAL*	1986
TANYA TUCKER	*GREATEST HITS*	1978
CONWAY TWITTY	*GREATEST HITS*	1981
CONWAY TWITTY	*GREATEST HITS VOL. 2*	1988
CONWAY TWITTY	*THE VERY BEST OF . . .*	1983
CONWAY TWITTY	*NUMBER ONES*	1988
CONWAY TWITTY & LORETTA LYNN	*THE VERY BEST OF . . .*	1988
ROGER WHITTAKER	*THE BEST OF . . .*	1980
DON WILLIAMS	*THE BEST OF . . . VOL. 2*	1980
HANK WILLIAMS	*GREATEST HITS*	1969
HANK WILLIAMS	*24 GREATEST HITS*	1977
HANK WILLIAMS JR.	*FAMILY TRADITION*	1983
HANK WILLIAMS JR.	*WHISKEY BENT & HELL BOUND*	1981

RELIGIOUS RECORDINGS

AMY GRANT	*MY FATHER'S EYES*	1987
AMY GRANT	*AGE TO AGE*	1983
DALLAS HOLM & PRAISE	*LIVE*	1984
SANDI PATTI	*MORE THAN WONDERFUL/LIVE*	1985
SANDI PATTI	*THE GIFT GOES ON*	1988
SANDI PATTI	*SONGS FROM THE HEART*	1987
SANDI PATTI	*HYMNS JUST FOR YOU*	1986
SANDI PATTI	*MORNING LIKE THIS*	1987
SANDI PATTI	*MAKE HIS PRAISE GLORIOUS*	1989
VARIOUS	*ALLELUIA - PRAISE GATHERING*	1971

♦ Apart from those listed, there are several **half-million selling Christmas albums** which never hit the pop charts (as there are separate Christmas LP charts). Among these are LPs by **Herb Alpert, Beach Boys, Glen Campbell, Nat 'King' Cole, Perry Como** (2), **Amy Grant, Henry Mancini, Dean Martin, Johnny Mathis, Mormon Tabernacle Choir** (3), **Jim Nabors, Partridge Family, Luciano Pavarotti, Elvis Presley** and **Andy Williams** (2).

♦ Despite the fact that neither of the records made the US charts, **Elmo & Patsy** earned gold discs in 1989 for their single and album entitled 'Grandma Got Run Over By A Reindeer', a seasonal favourite that had sold well every year since 1984.

♦ As with children's singles **children's albums** also occasionally go gold and again it's **Disney** who have the most with 15, including the million-sellers *Children's Favorites Vol I & II, Mousercise, Disney's Christmas Favorites* and the two million selling *Mickey Mouse Disco*.

HIT THAT PERFECT BEAT

UK SINGLES CHART FEATS

♦ Who has spent more weeks than any other act at the top of the UK chart in one year? No, it's not Elvis, the Beatles or Madonna – it's Frank Lovecchio, better known as **Frankie Laine**, who spent 26 weeks at the summit in 1953, 18 of them with 'I Believe' and eight with 'Answer Me'.

♦ **Dick Rowe**, known as 'the man who turned down the **Beatles**', produced the first vocal group to top the UK charts, the **Stargazers**, who were also the first British group to top it twice. This feat was not equalled by another vocal group until the arrival of the Beatles nine years later!

♦ The first artist to have as many as five different records in the UK singles chart at the same time was **Bill Haley** in 1955, and in 1957 **Elvis Presley** also scored five entries in the Top 20 with another two in the next ten.

♦ Skiffle King **Lonnie Donegan** is the only solo act to have achieved at least five different hits a year for five years running. He achieved this between 1956–60.

♦ The first act to see their first three records go to no. 1 was **Gerry & The Pacemakers** with 'How Do You Do It?', 'I Like It' and 'You'll Never Walk Alone' in 1963. **Frankie Goes To Hollywood** repeated this feat in 1984 with 'Relax', 'Two Tribes' and 'The Power Of Love' and in doing so sold twice as many records as Gerry. The hat trick was acheived again in 1989 by **Jive Bunny & The Mastermixers** with 'Swing The Mood', 'That's What I Like' and 'Let's Party'.

♦ The record for the most consecutive UK Top 10 hits with first chart records by a male artist is the 11 set by **Gary Glitter** in 1975.

♦ The only six-singles pack to make the UK Top 20 was the **Police**'s 'Six Pack' which reached no. 17 in 1980. Five of the singles were re-issues and the new release was 'The Bed's Too Big Without You'.

♦ **St. Winifred's School Choir** not only topped the UK chart with the single 'There's No One Quite Like Grandma' in 1980, but were also featured on the no. 1 hit by Brian & Michael, 'Matchstalk Men & Matchstalk Cats And Dogs' two years earlier.

♦ Apart from the **Beatles** the only other acts to have held the no. 1 and no. 2 spots on the chart simultaneously are **John Lennon** (with 'Imagine' and 'Happy Xmas War Is Over' in 1981), **Frankie**

*Rocker **Bill Haley** who clocked up five simultaneous singles in the British Top 20.*

Goes To Hollywood (with 'Two Tribes' and 'Relax' in 1984) and **Madonna** (with 'Into The Groove' and 'Holiday' in 1985).

♦ The **Smiths** once held the record for saturation of the UK indie chart when on 28th January, 1984, their first three releases held the Top 3 places. They were 'Hand In Glove', 'This Charming Man' and 'What Difference Does It Make'. The current indie chart saturation record is held by **Happy Mondays** who had six entries in that Top 30 in February, 1990.

♦ The only week that both the top two singles in the UK were new entries occurred on 15th December, 1984 when **Band Aid**'s 'Do They Know It's Christmas' came in at no. 1 and **Wham!**'s 'Last Christmas/Everything She Wants' entered in the runner-up position. Incidentally, **George Michael** was a featured artist on both of these records.

♦ **Midge Ure** holds the UK record for appearances in the singles chart with different groups. He has charted as a member of **Slik** in 1976, **Rich**

Kids in 1978, **Visage** and **Ultravox** in 1980 and **Band Aid** in 1984. In all, he appeared on 32 chart records in the 80s, which included his solo no. 1 'If I Was' in 1985.

♦ It was 13th time lucky for singer **Feargal Sharkey** when, in 1985, his 13th chart record 'A Good Heart' became his first UK no. 1. The song was written by **Maria McKee** who hit the top herself with another of her songs, 'Show Me Heaven', in 1990.

♦ The most simultaneous entries ever on the UK singles chart was by the **Jam** in 1985, who had an amazing 15 different records in the Top 75 shortly after they had split up.

♦ The first single to top the UK pop, indie and dance charts simultaneously was **M/A/R/R/S'** smash 'Pump Up The Volume', in 1987.

♦ The biggest jump ever in the UK Top 75 was made by **Nick Berry**'s single 'Every Loser Wins' which leapt from no. 66 to no. 4 in 1986. The biggest jump on the UK Top 200 singles chart (available only to the record business) was the 176 places from no. 182 to no. 6 made by **Erasure** with 'Drama', in September, 1989.

♦ The only act to have a Top 30 record in the UK in every year of the 80s was **Shakin' Stevens**, the leading figure of rock 'n' roll in that decade, who has yet to crack the US Top 40. Shaky has also appeared on BBC TV's *Top Of The Pops* over 50 times – a record beaten only by pop veteran **Cliff Richard**.

♦ **Simple Minds**' record 'Belfast Child' was not only at six minutes and thirty-nine seconds the longest running UK no. 1

*Britain's most regular chart visitor in the 80s was **Shakin' Stevens**, who must cry just a little when he thinks about his lack of US hits.*

since 'Hey Jude' by the **Beatles**, but it also broke the record for the highest entry by an EP when it came in at no. 2 in 1989. At the time it also broke the record for the fastest-selling CD single.

♦ **Elton John** was the third artist to notch up 50 separate UK chart entries – a feat he achieved in 1989, 18 years after his first hit. The previous two people to hit the half century were **Cliff Richard**, who hit the mark in 1969 (11 years after his first hit) and **Elvis Presley**, who made it in 1964, just eight years after first charting.

♦ The most new entries to the UK Top 75 chart happened on 19th May, 1990 when 25 new records appeared on the chart.

The most new entries in the UK Top 40 was ten, which occurred on 9th December, 1989.

♦ The first act to make the UK Top 40 with the same record in three separate years was **Bill Haley**, whose classic 'Rock Around The Clock' did the trick in 1955, '56 and '57. The next artist to do this was **Wink Martindale** with his 'Deck Of Cards' in 1959, '63 and '73. It was the only hit for the man who is now one of the top US TV quiz show hosts. The only other three-time UK hits were 'Leader Of The Pack' from the **Shangri-Las**, a Top 20 hit in 1965, '72 and '76, and 'You've Lost That Lovin' Feelin'' from the **Righteous Brothers**, a Top 20 hit in 1965, '69 and '90. Incidentally, this record is also the only track to have been on a number one record in the UK on three separate occasions. It topped the chart in its own right in 1965, hit no. 1 on the B-side of **Berlin**'s 12-inch of 'Take My Breath Away' in 1986, and was on the 12-inch version of the Brothers' 1990 chart-topper 'Unchained Melody'.

♦ The highest chart entry by a new name (ie an artist or group whose members have not charted before) in the UK was set in November, 1990, by US rapper **Vanilla Ice**, whose American chart-topper 'Ice Ice Baby' came in at no. 3 in its first week. Other newcomers who made the Top 5 in Britain in their first week were **neil** (Nigel Planer) with 'Hole In My Shoe' in 1984, **Bomb The Bass** with 'Beat Dis' in 1988, and **Partners In Kryme** with 'Turtle Power' in 1990.

♦ **Iron Maiden** became the first heavy metal act to enter the UK chart at no. 1, which they did with 'Bring Your Daughter . . . To The Slaughter' in its first week of release in 1991.

♦ The British group with the most singles chart entries (excluding re-issues) in Britain is not the **Beatles** or the **Stones** but **Status Quo**, who are still adding to their total of 41 that they have notched up since 1968. The Stones are second with 36, whilst the Beatles notched up 28.

US SINGLES CHART FEATS

♦ The record that has most frequently returned to the US Top 40 is **Bing Crosby**'s classic 'White Christmas' which scored in every year from 1942–62, excluding '52. From 1963 onwards there has been a separate Christmas chart in the US and it has appeared on it every year since. In Britain, where the single sold over a million copies, it only hit the Top 40 once, which was in 1977 – the year that Bing died.

♦ The first artist to hold the top two spots on the singles chart in the last forty years was **Johnny Ray**, who saw both sides of his

Did **Johnny Ray** *cry for joy in 1951?*

second single take those top two rungs in 1951. The songs concerned were 'Cry' and 'The Little White Cloud That Cried'.

♦ The first time that three British records appeared in the US Top 20 was not, as you may think, in the Swingin' 60s but in 1959. The records concerned were 'Petite Fleur' by **Chris Barber and his Jazz Band**, 'Manhattan Spiritual' by **Reg Owen and his Orchestra** and 'The Children's Marching Song' by **Cyril Stapleton and his Orchestra**.

♦ **Jimmy Gilmer**, who had a US no. 1 in 1963 with 'Sugar Shack', is now the southern regional head of **SBK Records** in the US. SBK are the label who gave us **Partners In Kryme**, **Vanilla Ice** and **Wilson Phillips**.

♦ **Hank Medress**, a member of the **Tokens**, who had a US no. 1 in 1961 with 'The Lion Sleeps Tonight', heads **EMI**'s music publishing company in Canada.

♦ The record for the most simultaneous entries on the US singles chart is 13, which was set in 1964 by the **Beatles** who beat the existing record of 10 singles which was set by **Elvis Presley** in his hey-day in 1956.

♦ The record for the highest entering single on the US Top 100 was set by the **Beatles** in 1970 when 'Let It Be' came in at no. 6.

♦ The highest entry by a 'new face' was 'Purple People Eater' by singer/actor **Sheb Wooley** which came in at no. 7 in 1958. In recent years the highest entry for a new artist is no. 27, set by **M.C. Hammer** with his 1990 hit 'U Can't Touch This'.

♦ The only record to go from no. 7 to no. 6 to no. 5 to no. 4 to no. 3 to no. 2 to no. 1 in consecutive weeks in the US was 'Gonna Fly Now' by **Bill Conti** which hit the top in 1977.

♦ The record with the longest title to make the US Top 20 was **Stars On 45** (known in the UK as **Starsound**) with 'Medley: Intro Venus/Sugar Sugar/No Reply/I'll Be Back/Drive My Car/Do You Want To Know A Secret/We Can Work It Out/I Should Have Known better/Nowhere Man/You're Going To Lose That Girl/Stars On 45' which hit no. 1 in 1981.

♦ **Ben E. King** is the only artist whose voice has been heard on Top 10 records in each of the last four decades in the US. In the 50s he sang the lead on the Drifters' 'There Goes My Baby'; in the 60s he scored with solo hits 'Stand By Me' and 'Spanish Harlem', in the 70s with 'Supernatural Thing' and in the 80s with the return of 'Stand By Me'.

♦ **Richard Marx** was the first male singer to see his first six releases go into the US Top 3. He completed this feat (which only **Whitney Houston** had succeeded in doing before) in August, 1989.

♦ In 1990 **Elton John** equalled Elvis Presley's record of having US Top 40 hits for 21 consecutive years. Elvis managed this feat between 1956–77 whilst Elton's run started in 1970.

UK LP FEATS

♦ The first **EMI** album to sell over 100 000 in the UK was *Black & White Minstrel Show* by the

*Four consecutive no. 1 album entries – that's a **Police** record.*

George Mitchell Minstrels in 1961. Two years later, an EMI album had 100 000 advance orders – it was the **Beatles'** *Please Please Me*.

♦ **James Last** holds the record for the most UK album chart entries with the least number of Top 10 hits. The German bandleader first charted in 1967 and to date has had 54 chart entries with only four having reached the Top 10.

♦ The record number of weeks spent on the UK LP chart is the 443 (8.5 years) by **Fleetwood Mac**'s *Rumours* which first entered the chart in 1977. Incidentally, **Mick Fleetwood**, the group's leader and one time member of the **Bo Street Runners**, surprisingly filed for bankruptcy in 1984 with debts of nearly $4 million and assets of just over $2 million.

♦ Third time lucky proved to be the case for **Peter Gabriel** whose third successive album with the title *Peter Gabriel* hit the no. 1 place in the UK in 1980. The previous two LPs had made the Top 10, as did his fourth album – surprisingly entitled *Peter Gabriel*!

♦ **Meat Loaf**'s *Deadringer* album set a record in 1981 when it became the first LP by an American act to hit no. 1 on the UK chart in its first week. It was the follow-up album to the classic *Bat Out Of Hell* LP which spent a staggering 176 weeks on the UK chart before reaching its peak position of no. 9. It then stayed on the chart for a further 219 weeks, making a total of 395 weeks (7.5 years) on the chart – the record for a US act! The first American to enter the UK chart at no. 1 with their debut album was **Terence Trent D'Arby** with his *Introducing The Hardline According To . . .* in 1987 (though this was recorded in the UK).

♦ The record number of simultaneous entries on the UK LP chart for a British act is 10, set by **David Bowie** in July, 1983.

♦ 'A **Police** record' was set in

Elton John *found that sleeping with the past made him a chart-topper of the present.*

1983 when the group became the first act to have four successive albums enter the UK chart at no. 1.

♦ Amongst the artists who have had multiple UK album chart entries are **Jim Reeves** who had eight in September 1964, **Elvis Presley** who had eight in September 1977, **Billy Joel** who had six entries in July 1984, **Bruce Springsteen** who had seven separate entries in June, 1985, **Dire Straits** who had six in February, 1986, and **Fleetwood Mac** who had five on the chart in May, 1988.

♦ It is not unusual for a double album to sell as well as a single one but there have never been more of them in the UK Top 40 than on 4th May, 1985, when 11 of the slots were taken by double LP sets. The first double LP to top the chart was the **Beatles'** *White Album* in 1968.

♦ Albums entering the US LP chart at no. 1 are a rarity but in Britain it is commonplace. The record number of albums doing this in succession is seven – it all started on 16th September, 1989. The LPs were: the **Original Cast** album of *Aspects of Love*, **Eurythmics'** *We Too Are One*, **Tina Turner'**s *Foreign Affair*, **Tracy Chapman'**s *Crossroads*, **Tears For Fears'** *The Seeds of Love*, **Kylie Minogue'**s *Enjoy Yourself* and **Erasure'**s *Wild*.

♦ The year with the most different no. 1 albums in the UK was 1989 when 27 separate LPs hit the top spot.

♦ **Soul II Soul** were the first black British act to top the UK album charts twice, and the first to simultaneously top the singles and albums charts, which they did in 1989. They are also the most successful British black group of all time in the US.

♦ Between February and April, 1990, the release of 12-inch versions of their old singles gave heavy metal group **Iron Maiden** ten different entries in the UK album Top 20.

♦ **Elton John** holds the UK record for the longest gap between no. 1 LPs. His *Greatest Hits* hit the top in 1975 and *Sleeping With The Past* got there 15 years and 6 months later.

♦ On 31st March, 1990, for the first time two classical recordings were in the UK Top 10 albums – they were violinist **Nigel Kennedy**'s *Vivaldi Four Seasons* and *The Essential Pavarotti* by Italian opera singer **Luciano Pavarotti**. The latter record also became the first classical record to top the chart – a feat Luciano, together with fellow opera singers **Placido Domingo** and **José Carreras**, repeated a couple of months later with their *In Concert* album.

♦ The only time that two albums accounted for over 600 000 sales in the UK in one week occurred on the week ending 24th November, 1990, when **Madonna**'s *The Immaculate Collection* sold over 340 000 and **Elton John**'s *The Very Best Of . . .* sold over 275 000 in those seven days.

♦ On 15th December, 1990, a record 34 compilation albums had places in the UK Top 100 albums.

US LP FEATS

♦ The first rock album to make the US charts was **Bill Haley**'s *Rock Around The Clock* which entered the listing on 23rd January, 1956.

♦ Apart from the **Beatles**, other acts who have simultaneously had two albums in the US Top 5 include this interesting and varied selection of artists: **Chubby Checker** (who also had four in the Top 10 and the no. 12 in 1962), **Herb Alpert** (who managed four in the Top 10 in 1966), **Roberta Flack**, **Iron Butterfly**, **Jim Croce**, **Allan Sherman**, **Simon & Garfunkel** (who had three in '68) and **Guns 'N Roses** in 1989.

♦ The only time the top four albums on the US chart were all comedy records occurred on 9th March, 1963 – the acts concerned were **Allan Sherman** (with two albums), **Frank Fontaine** and **Vaughn Meader**.

♦ The album that spent the most consecutive weeks in the US Top 40 was the soundtrack to *Dr Zhivago* which was there for 115 weeks back in 1966–7. Since then, the long-stay record is shared by **Bruce Springsteen** with *Born In The USA* (1985) and **Def Leppard** with *Hysteria* (1988), which both spent 96 consecutive weeks in the Top 40.

♦ **The Monkees** are the only act to have scored four different US no. 1 albums in one year. The year

U2 *had cause for celebration with the runaway success of their albums.*

was 1967 and the LPs were: *The Monkees*, *More Of The Monkees*, *Headquarters* and *Pisces, Aquarius, Capricorn & Jones Ltd.* Despite such a great start they never again hit the summit. The group also hold the record for the biggest jump to the no. 1 spot on the US LP chart – a massive 121 places for *More Of The Monkees* which had entered at no. 122.

♦ **Pink Floyd** spent a record-breaking 740 weeks (13.5 years) on the US Top 200 with *Dark Side Of The Moon* which, since its release in 1973, has sold over 11 million Stateside.

♦ **Led Zeppelin** joined the few acts to have had six albums simultaneously on the US chart when their entire output of albums charted on 29th March, 1975.

♦ It is thought that the biggest one-day sale of any album was that for the first day of the release of **Prince**'s *Purple Rain* in 1984, which is claimed to have sold 1.3 million in the US.

♦ The only box-set to top the chart was **Bruce Springsteen**'s *Live 1975–1985* in 1986. The five-album set hit no. 1 in its first

week on the chart.

♦ **U2** had the highest-entering LP by an act that had previously never been in the US Top 10 when, in May, 1987, their *The Joshua Tree* came into the Top 200 at no. 7. The album went on to sell over two million in the US in just six weeks. A year later this Irish group also had the fastest-selling double LP with their *Rattle & Hum* which sold over one million in its first week of release in the US in October 1988, not to mention 300 000 in its first week in the UK. It became the first double LP in eight years to top the US charts.

♦ The first all-metal US Top 3 albums occurred in July, 1988, when the leading trio were *OU812* by **Van Halen**, *Hysteria* by **Def Leppard** and *Appetite For Destruction* by **Guns 'N Roses**.

♦ The fastest-selling rap album of all time is **Vanilla Ice**'s *To The Extreme* which sold five million copies in its first 12 weeks in the US in late 1990. It is the fastest-selling LP since **Prince**'s *Purple Rain* which sold a record eight million in a mere 20 weeks in 1984.

ALL AROUND THE WORLD

BEATS INTERNATIONAL

♦ **Pink Floyd**'s UK no. 1 'Another Brick In The Wall' was banned in South Africa as it inspired a boycott of black schools.

♦ The first singer to enter the UK chart in two different groups in the same week was Belgium based **Ya Kid K** who appeared on the chart fronting both **Technotronic** and **Hi Tek 3** on 3rd February 1990.

♦ On 3rd February, 1990, a unique chart achievement occurred – the top three places on the UK singles chart were held by non-UK/US acts. The singles were: no. 1 – 'Nothing Compares 2 U' – **Sinead O'Connor** (from Ireland), no. 2 – 'Tears On My Pillow' by **Kylie Minogue** (from Australia) and no. 3 – 'Get Up' by **Technotronic** (from Belgium).

♦ The only Swedish acts to have topped the UK singles chart are **Abba** and **Europe**, who were both launched from the Eurovision song contest. Abba of course won the competition in 1975 with 'Waterloo' and Europe, then under the name The Force, were the Swedish entry in 1982.

Controversial hit-makers **Pink Floyd**.

Mark Knopfler - the man the kiwis love to see in **Dire Straits**.

♦ It is claimed that eight per cent of New Zealand's population saw **Dire Straits** when the group were on tour there in 1981.

♦ French artists' best week on the UK charts occurred on 1st October, 1977, when three acts nestled in the Top 10 – they were **Space** with 'Magic Fly', **Jean-Michel Jarre** with 'Oxygene Part IV' and **La Belle Epoque** with their revival of 'Black Is Black'.

♦ Australian acts had a moment of triumph when a record four singles were in the US Top 10 in November, 1981. The records concerned were 'Physical' by **Olivia Newton-John**, 'The Night Owls' from the **Little River Band**, 'Here I Am' by **Air Supply** and 'I've Done Everything For You' by **Rick Springfield**.

♦ Australian acts had their best spell ever on the UK charts in May, 1989, when they had six singles in the Top 75. The acts concerned were **Kylie Minogue**, **Midnight Oil**, **Jason Donovan**,

Inxs, **Stefan Dennis**, **1972** and **Lynne Hamilton**.

♦ In September, 1989, the UK dance chart was headed by three European acts – an unprecedented event. The acts were **Black Box** and **Sueno Latino**, both from Italy, and Belgium-based **Technotronic**.

♦ In Japan the most successful female singer is **Seiko Matsudo** who, it is claimed, has had a dozen consecutive no. 1 albums and two dozen consecutive chart topping singles! Her debut album in English speaking territories includes guest appearances by **George Michael**, **Gloria Estefan** and **Donnie Wahlberg** (from New Kids On The Block). As yet, no Japanese female singers have had a Top 40 US or UK hit; so it remains to be seen whether Seiko can break another record now that she has the power of the Japanese owned Sony/ Columbia (CBS) records behind her. She has also scored in Japan with a duet with **Placido**

Domingo called 'Till I Loved You' which he recorded with different vocal partners in different countries. In Europe he sang the track with **Jennifer Rush**, in the US it was with **Dionne Warwick** and in Spanish speaking countries the recording was with **Gloria Estefan**.

♦ In a poll amongst Russian teenagers in 1990, the acts they said they would most like to see perform were **Michael Jackson**, **Pink Floyd** and the **Beatles**.

♦ **Sinead O'Connor** was the first Irishwoman to top the UK album chart – she did it with *I Do Not Want What I Haven't Got*, in 1990.

♦ German group **Nena** topped the charts in their homeland, the

Olivia Newton-John *got physical and led the successful Australian invasion of the US charts in 1981.*

US, Australia and the UK in 1984 with '99 Luftballons'. In the first three countries it was the original German version that topped the chart but it took an English language version to do the job in the UK.

TRANSATLANTIC TRIALS

♦ It is common knowledge that over the last 26 years hundreds of British acts have hit in the US. It is such a common occurrence that you may find it hard to believe how little success the following top British recording acts have had on the US Top 20 singles chart.

NAME OF ACT	UK TOP 20s	US TOP 20s
STATUS QUO	36	1
THE SHADOWS	35*	0
SHAKIN' STEVENS	24*	0
ROXY MUSIC/ BRYAN FERRY	23	0
SLADE	22*	0
MADNESS	21	1
BILLY FURY	19	0
ADAM FAITH	16*	0
MARC BOLAN/T-REX	15*	1
SMITHS/MORRISSEY	15	0
SHOWADDYWADDY	15	0
SPANDAU BALLET	15	1
MUD	14*	0
CILLA BLACK	14*	0
JAM	13*	0
WINIFRED ATWELL	13	0
MAX BYGRAVES	13	0
TOMMY STEELE	13	0
DICKIE VALENTINE	13	0
ADAM & THE ANTS	12*	0
GARY GLITTER	12*	1

NAME OF ACT	UK TOP 20s	US TOP 20s
SHIRLEY BASSEY	12	1
KATE BUSH	12	0
ALMA COGAN	12	0
FIVE STAR	12	0
GARY NUMAN	12*	1
STRANGLERS	12	0
STYLE COUNCIL	12	0
BUCKS FIZZ	11	0
RUSS CONWAY	11	0
KYLIE MINOGUE	11*	1
RUBY MURRAY	11	0
SMALL FACES	11	1
SANDIE SHAW	10*	0
BONEY M	10*	0
DAVE DEE, DOZY, BEAKY, MICK & TICH	10	0
KIM WILDE	10	1
WIZZARD/ROY WOOD	10	0
BOOMTOWN RATS	9*	0
BROS	9*	0
MOVE	9	0
ALVIN STARDUST	9	0
JASON DONOVAN	9*	0
SUZI QUATRO	8*	1
SPECIALS	8	0
DARTS	8	0
SEX PISTOLS	7	0
FRANK IFIELD	5	1
FRANKIE GOES TO HOLLYWOOD	5	1
LEVEL 42	5	1
MARMALADE	5	1

* including no. 1 hit(s)

♦ This particular situation works both ways as this list of top US recording stars from the last few decades, who have either yet to hit the British Top 20 or, have only made one appearance, shows:

NAME OF ACT	US TOP 20s	UK TOP 20s
THREE DOG NIGHT	18	1
BROOK BENTON	16	0
BOB SEGER & THE SILVER BULLET BAND	15	0

NAME OF ACT	US TOP 20s	UK TOP 20s
JOHN COUGAR MELLENCAMP	14	0
JOHNNY RIVERS	13	0
JOURNEY	12	0
PATTI PAGE	12	1
HELEN REDDY	11	1
PAUL REVERE & THE RAIDERS	11	0
DOOBIE BROTHERS	10	0
IMPRESSIONS	10	1
GARY LEWIS & THE PLAYBOYS	10	0
LITTLE RIVER BAND	10	0
LINDA RONSTADT (solo)	10	0
AIR SUPPLY	9	1
JERRY BUTLER	9	0
JOHN DENVER	9	1
TOMMY JAMES & THE SHONDELLS	9	1
RICHARD MARX	9	1
RICK SPRINGFIELD	9	0
YOUNG RASCALS	9	1
AMERICA	8	1
EXPOSE	8	0
LESLEY GORE	8	1
GUESS WHO	8	1
JAY & THE AMERICANS	8	0
KENNY LOGGINS	8	1
ANNE MURRAY	8	0
STYX	8	1
B.J. THOMAS	8	0
BRYAN ADAMS	7	1
ANDY GIBB	7	1
SHIRELLES	7	1
JAMES TAYLOR	7	1
JAN & DEAN	7	0

NAME OF ACT	FIRST US HIT	FIRST UK HIT (TOP 20)
AEROSMITH	1973	1989
BRYAN ADAMS	1982	1985
ASHFORD & SIMPSON	1973	1985
JAMES BROWN	1956	1966
CAMEO	1977	1985
RAY CHARLES	1949	1961
CHUBBY CHECKER	1959	1961
NEIL DIAMOND	1966	1970
DRIFTERS	1953	1960
EARTH, WIND & FIRE	1971	1977
FOUR TOPS	1964	1967
MARVIN GAYE	1962	1969
HEART	1976	1987
ISLEY BROTHERS	1959	1968
JEFFERSON AIRPLANE/ STARSHIP	1967	1985
B.B. KING	1951	1989
BEN E. KING	1960	1987
KISS	1974	1987
GLADYS KNIGHT	1961	1967
KOOL & THE GANG	1969	1979
PATTI LABELLE	1962	1975
HUEY LEWIS	1982	1985
BETTE MIDLER	1972	1989
MIRACLES	1959	1969
JOHNNY NASH	1957	1968
POINTER SISTERS	1973	1981
PRINCE	1978	1984
OTIS REDDING	1963	1965
REO SPEEDWAGON	1977	1981
BRUCE SPRINGSTEEN	1975	1985
BARBRA STREISAND	1964	1966
TEMPTATIONS	1962	1966
THREE DEGREES	1965	1974
TINA TURNER	1960	1966
VAN HALEN	1978	1984
LUTHER VANDROSS	1976	1987
STEVIE WONDER	1963	1966
ZZ TOP	1972	1984

♦ It is evident that success on one side of the Atlantic does not automatically mean success on the other and many a household name has had to wait years before finally becoming a transatlantic success. Amongst the American acts who probably thought they would never make it in Britain are:

♦ It is also worth remembering that early UK releases from American teenage sensations, like **Ricky Nelson** in the 50s, the **Monkees** in the 60s, the **Osmonds** and **Partridge Family** in the 70s and **New Kids On The Block** in the 80s, all failed to chart for these acts who, in time, became as big on both sides of the Atlantic. Quite often though, an American record will take the fancy of British record buyers and yet leave the American audience cold or at best luke warm, if it even merits a release in the US. Good examples of this phenomenon are:

and 'Inside Out'. Their transatlantic charter was 'Native New Yorker'.

♦ Another New York based dance act **Break Machine** also found the grass was greener on the other side of the Atlantic. This act, who failed to chart Stateside, had two UK Top 10s in 1984 with 'Street Dance', and 'Break Dance Party'.

♦ Yet another New York act that fared better across the Atlantic was **Kid Creole & The Coconuts**. This unique act chalked up seven UK charters including three UK Top 10 hits:

TITLE	ARTIST	UK PEAK	US PEAK
'THE FIRST TIME'	ROBIN BECK	1	–
'I NEED YOU'	BVSMP	3	–
'THE CROWN'	GARY BYRD	6	–
'ONE DAY I'LL FLY AWAY'	RANDY CRAWFORD	2	–
'ALMAZ'	RANDY CRAWFORD	4	–
'JACK YOUR BODY'	STEVE 'SILK' HURLEY	1	–
'ONE DAY IN YOUR LIFE'	MICHAEL JACKSON	1	55
'JUMP TO THE BEAT'	STACY LATTISAW	3	–
'INTO THE GROOVE'	MADONNA	1	–
'THEME FROM 'MASH''	MASH	1	–
'FULL METAL JACKET'	ABIGAIL MEAD & NIGEL GOULDING	2	–
'MOVE CLOSER'	PHYLLIS NELSON	1	–
'CANDY GIRL'	NEW EDITION	1	46
'LOVE TOWN'	BOOKER NEWBERRY III	6	–
'WALKING ON SUNSHINE'	ROCKER'S REVENGE	4	–
'CHAIN REACTION'	DIANA ROSS	1	66
'MY BABY JUST CARES FOR ME'	NINA SIMONE	5	–
'FRANKIE'	SISTER SLEDGE	1	75
'LATELY'	STEVIE WONDER	3	64

♦ New York based dance music trio **Odyssey** had the distinction of scoring five UK Top 10 hits of which only one made the Top 100 in their homeland. The British-only smashes were the no. 1 'Use It Up And Wear It Out', and the hits 'If You're Lookin' For A Way Out', 'Going Back To My Roots'

'I'm A Wonderful Thing, Baby', 'Stool Pigeon' and 'Annie I'm Not Your Daddy' but never once entered the US Top 100.

♦ Chicago's dance act **Inner City** have experienced the same fate, scoring three Top 10s in the UK with 'Big Fun', 'Good Life' and 'Ain't Nobody Better', yet the group has been unable to crack the Top 100 in its homeland.

♦ US TV spin-off group **The Kids From Fame** never managed to get a single into the US Top 100 yet had two Top 10s in Britain, in 1982, with 'Hi-Fidelity' and 'Starmaker'. This act also had five UK hit albums including three Top 10 entries but only peaked on the US chart at no. 98!

ATLANTIC CROSSING

♦ Apart from the **Beatles**, **Herman's Hermits** are the only British act to have had three records simultaneously in the US Top 20. This happened on 12th June, 1965, and the hits were: 'Wonderful World', 'Mrs. Brown You've Got A Lovely Daughter' and 'Silhouettes'.

♦ Amongst the achievements of **Barry Manilow** is the fact that he is the only artist to top both the US and UK album charts with different live LPs, neither of which even charted in the other country! They were *Barry Manilow Live* (US, 1977) and *Barry Live In Britain* (UK, 1982).

♦ **Un-American Top 100** – the record number of non-Americans on the US Top 100 occurred on 27th August, 1983, when 55.5 per cent of the acts were born outside the US, and of these 37.5 per cent were British (this increased to 40 per cent in April, 1984). Incidentally, on 8th May, 1985, British acts accounted for nine of

Against all odds – Englishman **Phil Collins** *holds the American record for the most Top 40 single hits in the 80s.*

the first ten places on the US chart – a feat that had only happened once before, in April, 1965.

♦ The record number of successive US no. 1s by foreign artists is eight – set between May and August, 1985. The acts concerned were: **Simple Minds**, **Wham!**, **Tears For Fears** (twice), **Bryan Adams**, **Phil Collins**, **Duran Duran** and **Paul Young**.

♦ What is the biggest-selling album ever by an all British group in the US? No, it's not by the Stones or the Beatles, but by Sheffield's own **Def Leppard** whose 1987 LP *Hysteria* has passed the nine million sales mark there.

♦ **Fleetwood Mac** first charted in the UK in 1968 and in the US in 1970. However, it took until November, 1987, before any of their many hit singles made *both* countries' Top 5. The record that finally did it for them was 'Little Lies'.

♦ The record for appearances in the US Top 40 in the 80s is held by the UK's **Phil Collins**, who appeared on 25 Top 40s in that decade. His colleague in Genesis, **Mike Rutherford**, is the only person to have US no. 1 hits in the 80s as a member of two different groups. With **Genesis** he had 'Invisible Touch' in 1986, and his own group **Mike & The Mechanics** hit the top with 'The Living Years' in 1989.

♦ The first UK act to top the black music chart in the US was **Carl Douglas**, who hit in 1975 with 'Kung Fu Fighting'. The second act to make it was **Paul McCartney** with his duet with **Michael Jackson**, 'The Girl Is Mine', in 1983. The first British group to achieve this feat was **Loose Ends** in 1985 with 'Hangin' On A String (Contemplating)'. The first solo female to top that chart was **Ruby Turner**, who scored in 1990 with 'It's Gonna Be Alright'. A month later, Britain's **Lisa Stansfield** reached the top with 'All Around The World' and shortly afterwards she had a second chart topper with 'You Can't Deny It'.

♦ The first act from Liverpool to make the American Top 10 was not, as you might think, the **Beatles**, but singer/songwriter and ex-holiday camp entertainer **Russ Hamilton**, who accomplished it in 1957 with his self-penned song 'Rainbow'.

♦ 'H' of course stands for 'hit' and three hits that had 'H' as their first letter and hit first on the US Hot Hundred before they hit in their homeland were **Simply Red**'s 'Holding Back The Years' in 1985, **T'Pau**'s 'Heart And Soul' in 1987, and **Breathe**'s 'Hands To Heaven' in 1988.

♦ Two of the four most charted groups in British record history are virtually unknown in the US. They are **Status Quo** and the **Shadows**, who trail just behind the **Beatles** and the **Rolling Stones** in terms of different singles on the chart.

♦ It's hard to believe that in the sexually liberated Britain of the 80s, two big hits had to have their titles amended for mention on the radio so as not to cause upset. The records were 'We Don't Have To' (known in the US as 'We Don't Have To Take Our Clothes Off') by **Jermaine Stewart** and '(Sexual) Healing' by the late **Marvin Gaye**, which went without the brackets Stateside.

HAPPY BIRTHDAY

Ever wondered what important musical events have occurred on the birthdays of well-known acts? Look no further . . .

♦ On **Madonna**'s birthday – 16th August (1958):
Al Hibbler, who had the original hit with 'Unchained Melody' was born (1915) . . . **Eydie Gorme** of 'Blame It On The Bossa Nova' fame was born (1931) . . . **Ketty Lester**, who hit with 'Love Letters' in 1962, was born (1934) . . . R&B singer **Barbara George**, who hit in 1961 with 'I Know', was born (1942) . . . **Barry Hay**, the leader of top Dutch rock band Golden Earring, was born (1948) . . . **James 'J.T.' Taylor**, the vocalist with Kool & The Gang, was born (1953) . . . The **Beatles** sacked drummer **Pete Best** (1962) . . . **MC Remedee** of the Cookie Crew was born (1967) . . . The **Ramones** made their debut at New York's CBGB club (1974) . . . **Peter Gabriel** left Genesis (1975) . . . **Cliff Richard** started a Russian tour (1976) . . . **Elvis Presley** and opera star **Maria Callas** died (1977) . . . **Bill Ward** left Black Sabbath, **Jools Holland** left Squeeze, **Jah Wobble** left PIL and **Cozy Powell** left Rainbow (all in 1980) . . . **Bad News** debuted at Castle Donnington (1986) . . . **Sports Aid** held a concert at Sheffield United's football ground (1988).

♦ On **Elvis Presley**'s birthday – 8th January (1935):
Shirley Bassey was born (1937) . . . **Little Anthony** (Gourdine) leader of the Imperials was born (1941) . . . **David Bowie** was born (1947) . . . **Mike Reno** leader of Loverboy was born (1955) . . . Elvis' *Milk Cow Boogie* was released but failed to chart (1955) . . . **Buddy Holly**'s US Tour with the **Everly Brothers** started (1958) . . . **Eddie Cochran** recorded *Three Steps To Heaven* at his very last session (1960) . . . **Bandstand** (a US pop TV programme) hosted an 'Elvis Special' on which he did not appear (1962) . . . The last 'Shindig' show was seen – it starred the **Kinks** and the **Who** (1966) . . . **Paul Weller** joined Polydor (1983) . . . **Ozzy Osbourne** started an eight month US tour (1984) . . . The Post Office issued Elvis Presley stamps to celebrate his 50th birthday (1985).

♦ On **John Lennon**'s birthday – 9th October (1940):
Soul singer **O.V. Wright** was born (1939) – he died 3 weeks before John Lennon . . . **John Entwistle** of The Who was born (1944) . . . **Jackson Browne** was born (1948) . . . **Eddie Cochran** recorded 'Let's Get Together' (the original of 'C'mon Everybody') (1958) . . . Top UK radio show *Saturday Club* started (1959) . . .

John Lennon *first met* Yoko *on his birthday.*

John first met **Yoko** (1966) . . . Famous revolutionary **Che Guevara** was killed (1967) . . . **Elvis Presley** divorced Priscilla (1973) . . . **Gary Glitter** was declared bankrupt (1980) . . . **Aztec Camera** signed to WEA (1983) . . . 'The Hitman Roadshow' launched by PWL Records and starring **Kylie Minogue** and **Sonia** started (1989).

♦ On **Paul McCartney**'s birthday – 18th June (1942): **Johnny Pearson** leader of Sounds Orchestral and the Top Of The Pops orchestra was born (1925) . . . **Tommy Hunt**, lead singer of the Flamingos, was born

(1933) . . . **Don 'Sugar Cane' Harris** of the R&B duo Don & Dewey was born (1938) . . . The 'first British rock star' **Tommy Steele** got married (1960) . . . **Alison Moyet** was born (1961) . . . **Culture Club**'s first tour started in Manchester (1982) . . . **Pigbag** split up (1983) . . . **Judas Priest**'s fans rioted at the Madison Square Gardens (1984).

♦ On **Elton John**'s birthday – 25th March (1947): Fifties country star **Bonnie Guitar** was born (1933) . . . The late **Johnny Burnette**, who had the original hit of 'You're 16' in 1961, was born (1934) . . . The first 'hillbilly' chart was introduced in *Billboard* – it later became the 'country' chart (1939) . . . **Anita Bryant**, who had the original of 'Paper Roses' in 1960, was born (1940) . . . **Aretha Franklin** was born (1942) . . . **John Rowles**, who hit with 'If I Only Had Time' in 1968, was born (1947) . . . **Elvis Presley** made his last appearance on the *Dorsey Brothers* TV show and sang 'Heartbreak Hotel' (1956) . . . **Buddy Holly** played his last British date (1958) . . . **Elvis** made his last live appearance for 8 years (1961) . . . The **Beatles** first appeared on *Top Of The Pops* (1964) . . . **Tracie** (Young), who hit with 'The House That Jack Built' in 1983, was born (1965) . . . British bandleader **Billy Cotton** died (1969) . . . **Bros**' documentary *The Story So Far* was shown on British TV (1988) . . .

♦ On **Michael Jackson**'s birthday – 29th August (1958): Outstanding jazz musician **Charlie Parker** was born (1920) . . . Blues/jazz great **Dinah Washington** was born Ruth Lee Jones (1924) . . . Top UK comedian **Lenny Henry** was born (1958) . . . The (Silver) **Beatles** performed their first live show with **George Harrison** (1958) . . . **Eddi Sadenia** (née **Reader**), ex-leader of Fairground Attraction, was born (1959) . . . **Herman's Hermits** had their first press review (1964) . . . The **Beatles** performed their last US show (1966) – it was in San Francisco . . . R&B great **Jimmy Reed** died (1976) . . . The **Clash** played their first public gig . . . Three people were arrested for trying to steal **Elvis Presley**'s corpse (1977) . . . **Stevie Wonder** began a successful week at Wembley (1987).

♦ On **George Michael**'s birthday – 25th June (1963): The **Battle Of Little Big Horn** took place (1876) . . . Top Cajun performer **Clifton Chenier** was born (1925) . . . Soul singer **Eddie Floyd** was born (1935) . . . **Carly Simon** was born (1945) . . . The **Korean War** started (1950) . . . **Tim Finn**, leader of top New Zealand rock band Split Enz, was born (1952) . . . **David Paich** of Toto was born (1954) . . . The **Beatles** were seen worldwide thanks to a satellite TV link singing *All You Need Is Love* (1967) . . . The **Rolling Stones** played their first UK gig for six years to 72000 fans at Wembley (1982) . . . For the first time ever there were more foreign than American records on the US Top 100 (1983) . . . **Bruce Springsteen** played at Wembley (1988).

♦ On **Christmas Day**: Top entertianer **Cab Calloway** was born (1907) . . . Top MOR singer **Tony Martin** was born (1912) . . . R&B singers **Chris Kenner**, who wrote 'Land Of A 1000 Dances' and **Billy Horton**, leader of The Silhouettes of 'Get A Job' fame, were born (1929) . . . **O'Kelly Isley** of the Isley Brothers was born (1937) . . . Critically acclaimed producer **Phil Spector** was born (1940) . . . Country rock star **Jimmy Buffett** was born (1946) . . . Leading country singer **Barbara Mandrell** was born (1948) . . . **Annie Lennox** of the Eurythmics and country star **Steve Wariner** were born (1954) . . . The Pogues photogenic front man **Shane McGowan** was born (1958) . . . **Paul McCartney** announced his engagement to **Jane Asher** (1967) – it was called off eight months later.

I AM WOMAN

FEMALE FACTS AND FEATS

♦ The only female singer to have five different records on the UK chart at one time was Ireland's **Ruby Murray** in 1955. In recent years the only singer to come close was **Madonna**, who on 17th August, 1985, had a total of three singles in the UK Top 20: 'Into The Groove', 'Holiday' and 'Crazy For You'.

♦ **Connie Francis** had nine successive 'flops' on **MGM** and in the last 15 minutes of her supposed last session for the label she recorded a version of her father's favourite song, 'Who's

Connie Francis - *the first female LP chart-topper in Britain hit the top with 20 greats from 20 years before.*

Sorry Now' (she had kept promising him that she would record it even though she did not like the song herself). In 1958 it was this track which gave her the first of 56 hits in the US.

♦ The first female singer to sell a million copies of a single in the UK was American **Jennifer Rush** whose song 'The Power Of Love' passed that mark in 1985. The record, which had originally been a massive hit in Germany, surprisingly never made the Top 40 in her homeland.

♦ Mum's the word . . . Scottish housewife and mother of two Mary Sandeman's one-off no. 1 UK hit in 1981 'Japanese Boy' (recorded under the name **Aneka**) was rejected for release by her Japanese record company for being 'too Chinese'. Another mother of two, **Liz Hewson** gave her first live performance at the age of 38 on *Top Of The Pops* as singer in her husband's studio act the **Rah Band**. She had recorded the vocal to their Top 10 hit 'Clouds Across The Moon' in the back room studio in their house.

♦ In March, 1986, there were a record 11 solo female acts in the UK Top 40 LP chart.

♦ Amazingly, it took until August, 1977, before a female artist topped the UK album chart and the act who did it had not had

Does **Madonna** *cherish all the records she has broken?*

a no. 1 single for 19 years. She was **Connie Francis** and the record was *Twenty All Time Greats*. The first British girl to top the UK album chart was **Kate Bush** with *Never for Ever* in 1980. The first female to top the UK LP chart with her *debut* album was **Tracy Chapman** with her eponymous LP in 1988 – 30 years after the first chart was published. **Kylie Minogue**, the second female to accomplish this feat, did so just weeks later with her *Kylie* LP.

♦ The first time black female acts took the US Top 3 album places was on 21st June, 1986 when *Whitney Houston* by **Whitney Houston**, *Winner In You* by **Patti Labelle** and *Control* from **Janet Jackson** headed the chart.

♦ The first time female singers took the Top 3 singles places in the US was on 18th October, 1986, when the Top 3 records were 'When I Think Of You' by **Janet Jackson**, 'Typical Male' from **Tina Turner** and 'True Colors' by **Cyndi Lauper**.

♦ The first time the UK Top 5 singles were sung by females was on 22nd November, 1986. The ladies concerned were **Terri Nunn** of **Berlin** ('Take My Breath Away'), **Kim Wilde** ('You Keep Me Hangin' On'), the **Bangles** ('Walk Like An Egyptian'), **Mel & Kim** ('Showing Out') and **Corrine Drewery** of **Swing Out Sister** ('Breakout').

♦ **Madonna** was first US female singer to enter UK LP chart at no. 1 – she did it with *True Blue* in 1986.

♦ The only female artist to enter the US chart at no. 1 was **Whitney Houston** with her LP

Record-breaking **Kylie Minogue** *almost beat Tracy Chapman to an album record – she should be so lucky.*

Whitney in 1987. Whitney was also the first black female artist to top the UK LP chart and the first female to enter both the UK and US album chart at no. 1.

♦ 1st August, 1987 was the first day for over 32 years that the US Top 10 was dominated by women. The ladies concerned were: **Ann** and **Nancy Wilson** (of Heart), **Gloria Estefan**, **Carol Decker** (of T'Pau), **Kathy**, **Elizabeth** and **Moana Wolfgramm** (of The Jets), **Suzanne Vega** and **Whitney Houston**.

◆ **Carly Simon** has UK Top 10 hits in five-year cycles. She first did it in 1972 with 'You're So Vain', returned in 1977 with 'Nobody Does It Better', was back in 1982 with 'Why' and last hit the Top 10 in 1987 with 'Coming Around Again'. Watch out for her coming around again in 1992!

◆ It took over 35 years of UK charts before the first female trio of successive no. 1s happened. It was on the 20th February, 1988 that **Kylie Minogue** completed this triple feat with 'I Should Be So Lucky' which followed **Tiffany**'s 'I Think We're Alone Now', which was preceded by 'Heaven Is A Place On Earth' from **Belinda Carlisle**. Amazingly, later that year the feat was repeated – this time the artists concerned were **Robin Beck** ('First Time'), **Enya** ('Orinoco Flow') and **Whitney Houston** ('One Moment In Time'). Perhaps surprisingly, none of these six female artists was British.

◆ On 2nd April, 1988, a record 13 different female acts were present in the UK Top 40: **Tiffany**, **Sinitta**, **Kylie Minogue**, **Debbie Gibson**, **Whitney Houston**, **Belinda Carlisle**, **Vanessa Paradis**, **Taja Seville**, **Taylor Dayne**, **Pebbles**, **Natalie Cole**, **Hazel Dean** and **Brenda Russell**.

◆ **Whitney Houston** is the only artist to have had seven consecutive US no. 1 singles – an accomplishment not achieved even by the **Beatles** at their height. The singles were 'Saving All My Love For You' (1985), 'How Will I Know' and 'Greatest Love Of All' (1986), 'I Wanna Dance With Somebody' and 'Didn't We Almost Have It All' (1987) and 'So Emotional' and 'Where Do Broken Hearts Go' (1988).

◆ Choreographer turned singer **Paula Abdul** became the first artist ever to have four US no. 1 singles from a debut album. The tracks concerned were 'Straight Up', 'Forever Your Girl', 'Cold Hearted' and 'Opposites Attract', all taken from her first album *Forever Your Girl*, released in 1989.

◆ The first time female acts occupied the top four places on

Straight up, **Paula Abdul** *was the first person to have four US no. 1s from her debut album.*

the UK LP chart was on 14th October, 1989. The ladies concerned were **Kylie Minogue** (*Kylie*), **Tracy Chapman** (*Crossroads*), **Tina Turner** (*Foreign Affair*) and **Gloria Estefan** (*Cuts Both Ways*).

♦ As yet, no female artist has entered the UK chart at no. 1, but two have had singles make their debut in the runner-up position. They were **Madonna** with her 'Like A Prayer' and 'Crazy For You (remix)' and **Kylie Minogue** who has entered at no. 2 with 'The Loco-Motion', 'Hand On Your Heart', 'Wouldn't Change A Thing', 'Tears On My Pillow' and her duet with **Jason Donovan**, 'Especially For You'.

♦ **Bananarama** are the most successful British female group ever with 20 Top 40 entries between 1982–90 although, despite record company claims to the contrary, they trail behind the **Supremes** (who had a total of 29 British Top 40 hits) as the most successful female chart group of all time in the UK.

♦ On 17th February, 1990 three female trios appeared together in the US Top 10 for the first time. The records concerned were 'Two To Make It Right' by **Seduction**, 'Tell Me Why' by **Expose** and 'We Can't Go Wrong' by the **Cover Girls**.

♦ Also on 17th February, 1990 a record *nine* of the Top 10 records in the UK featured female singers.

♦ Women achieved the total US chart sweep on 24th March, 1990 – the records concerned were 'Black Velvet' by **Alannah Myles**, 'Love Will Lead You Back' by **Taylor Dayne** and 'Escapade' by **Janet Jackson** which headed the singles chart. The top two albums were *Forever Your Girl* by **Paula**

Abdul and *Rhythm Nation 1814* by **Janet Jackson**. A month later **Paula** and **Janet** were joined in the Top 4 by **Bonnie Raitt** and **Sinead O'Connor**.

♦ In January, 1991 **Janet Jackson** became the first artist to have seven Top 5 hits from one album. The album was *Rhythm Nation 1814* and the seven singles were 'Miss You Much', 'Rhythm Nation', 'Escapade', 'Alright', 'Come Back To Me', 'Black Cat', and 'Love Will Never Do (Without You)'. This meant that she had scored 12 Top 5 hits from just two albums – another first.

♦ The first time *new* female singers took the Top 3 singles places in the US was in May, 1990 when two British girls – **Sinead O'Connor** ('Nothing Compares 2 U') and **Lisa Stansfield** ('All Around The World') were joined by Canadian **Jane Child** ('Don't Wanna Fall In Love'). Incidentally, **Sinead** and **Jane** also produced their hits – which set another record.

♦ The two hottest female trios in US singles history are the **Supremes** and **Expose** both of whom chalked up seven Top 10 hits in just two years. The Supremes did it between 1965–67 and Expose between 1987–90. Incidentally, Expose were the first US group to have four Top 10 singles on one LP. The *Exposure* album (1988) amazingly only managed to reach no. 16 on the US chart.

♦ The female with most US no. 1s is **Madonna** whose 'Justify My Love' (1991) became her ninth no. 1, putting her one ahead of **Whitney Houston**. However, both of these acts are so hot that by now this record has probably changed hands a few times!

IN THE COUNTRY

COUNTRY GREATS

♦ The first country million-seller came in 1924 and was **Vernon Dalhart**'s 'The Wreck Of The Old 97'.

♦ The first black artist on the Grand Ole Opry (the famous country music show in Nashville, USA) was the 4ft 10in harmonica player **Deford Bailey** who appeared on the revered country music programme from Nashville on 19th June, 1926. When Deford's career began to nosedive he shined shoes near the Ryman Auditorium, where the show was recorded.

♦ The first Nashville recording is said to be **Sheb Wooley**'s 'Oklahoma Honky Tonk Gal' in 1945 on Bullet Records. Later in life, Sheb played Pete Nolan in the TV series *Rawhide*, wrote the theme to TV's *Hee Haw* and had a million-selling transatlantic hit with 'Purple People Eater'.

♦ The first country show in New York took place at the Carnegie Hall on 18th September, 1947, and it starred **Ernest Tubb** and **Minnie Pearl**, amongst others.

♦ Country music great **Hank Williams** had the top two country singles of the year in 1953 (the year he died aged 29), 'Kaw-Liga' and 'Your Cheatin' Heart'. This feat was not repeated until 1989

when newcomer **Clint Black** had the year's two biggest country hits with 'Better Man' and 'Killin' Time'.

♦ Country singer **Bobby Bare** should have had a no. 2 US hit in 1958 but his record 'All American Boy' was accidentally credited to the performer on the B-side – his friend **Bill Parsons**.

♦ In November, 1961, **Jimmy Rodgers**, **Hank Williams** and **Fred Rose** became the first artists inducted into the newly formed 'Country Music Hall of Fame'.

♦ Five of the most successful US country music singers in the UK over the years have been **Jim Reeves**, **Slim Whitman**, **Boxcar Willie**, **Tammy Wynette** and **Billie Jo Spears**. In total they have achieved 32 Top 20 albums and 25 Top 20 singles in Britain, yet in their homeland they have only scored two Top 20 LPs and three Top 20 singles between them.

♦ The first US country LP chart was introduced in 1964 and the first topper was *Ring Of Fire – The Best Of Johnny Cash*.

♦ The late **Jim Reeves** holds the UK record for having the most albums in the Top 20 simultaneously which he set posthumously in 1964 when eight of his records held down places equalling 40 per cent of the chart!

♦ The first (and only) major black artist in the country music field is **Charley Pride** who has scored over 60 country hits since first charting in 1966, including an amazing 29 no. 1s.

♦ On 19th April, 1980, the US country chart long dominated by male singers had a top five acts of **Crystal Gayle**, **Dottie West**, **Debby Boone**, **Emmylou Harris** and **Tammy Wynette** (who duetted with **George Jones**).

♦ Veteran R&B performer **Ray Charles** was voted by *Billboard* to be the Second Top New Country Act of 1983 – which was 34 years after his first recording and 21 years after he topped the charts with his album *Modern Sounds In Country And Western Music*. Incidentally, Ray has had chart

hits in the US in each of the last five decades.

♦ The only album to top the country chart in its first week of release was **George Strait**'s *Ocean Front Property* in 1987.

♦ The album that has spent the most weeks at the top of the US country chart since it started over 25 years ago is **Randy Travis**' *Always & Forever* which had 43 weeks at the top in 1988.

♦ **Reba McEntire** broke the record for the most weeks at the top of the US country chart by a female in September, 1989, when her album *Sweet 16* remained at the summit for its 11th week.

♦ Irish country singer **Daniel O'Donnell** held the top four places on the UK country album chart in April, 1990 – a record no performer has equalled.

TRAGEDY

DEATH ON DISC

♦ Over the years there have been many records about the deaths of loved ones, planned suicides and about death in general (in wars, etc.) that are very moving and done in good taste. However, there are other recordings which many people would say were the products of a 'sick' mind – those which tell

grisly and gruesome tales about one or more people, or animals, 'meeting their maker'. Sometimes these records attract the attention of the media and go on to be big hits – 'Tell Laura I Love Her', 'Teen Angel' and 'Leader Of The Pack', for example. Most of the following gory greats, for one reason or another 'stiffed' or 'died a death' (music jargon for flopped).

GROUP	RECORD
BILL ANDERSON	'The Last Mrs. Jones' Man who murdered his first wife tells his second wife of his plans to do the same to her.
BLOODROCK	'D.O.A.' Boy's thoughts as he and his girlfriend slowly die in the ambulance on the way to hospital after a plane crash.
JOANN BONN	'It May Kill Me' Murderess sings about her crime and the electric chair.
BUOYS	'Timothy' Trapped potholers have to eat one of their party to survive.
CHILL WILLS	'Daddy's Girl' Daughter and granddaughter die prematurely and are buried together by the grandfather.
JIMMY CROSS	'I Want My Baby Back' Dead girl is joined in her coffin by her boyfriend who can't live without her.
JIMMY DEAN	'When Judy Smiled' After his girlfriend's untimely death he commits suicide.
FIVE MAN ELECTRIC BAND	'Werewolf' Father armed with silver bullets sets out to kill his werewolf son but the son is victorious, which pleases the mother.
FERLIN HUSKY	'The Drunken Driver' Drunk father runs over and kills his two children.
LORENE MANN	'Hide My Sin' (A-B-O-R-T-I-O-N N-E-W Y-O-R-K) She spells out what her forthcoming abortion means to her.
DOLLY PARTON	'Two Little Orphans' After mom and dad's death the two children freeze to death on the stairs of the church.
RAY SAWYER	'Daddy's Little Girl' His young daughter's premonition of early death came true.
RAY SCOTT	'The Prayer' Black man prays that the racist governor of Alabama will die in various gruesome ways which he describes vividly.
THE SWEET SICK TEENS	'Agnes' Girlfriend is killed in the electric chair for spying.
PORTER WAGONER & DOLLY PARTON	'The Party' Two children are killed in a fire at home whilst the parents are out at a party. They promised the kids they would take them to church the next day which they do – to bury them.

GROUP	RECORD
DAVID WALSH	'Seven New Stars' A tribute to the seven people killed on the space shuttle.
Also: JOHNNY CYMBAL	'The Water Was Red' Girlfriend was eaten by a shark.
INCREDIBLE BROADSIDE BRASS BED BAND	'Little Dead Surfer Girl' As above, except that bit by bit her body washes up on the shore.
JACK KITTRELL	'Psycho' Man tells his mother he has killed his girlfriend, her lover, the child next door and his puppy and then he kills her.

LIVE FAST, DIE YOUNG

♦ It's sad to see how many artists have died before they even reached middle age. These are some of the most important artists to have passed on before they reached 35. If they were group members or were better known outside the pop music mainstream, the fact is mentioned in brackets.

ACT	AGE DIED	CAUSE OF DEATH
RITCHIE VALENS	17 years 9 months	Plane crash
EDDIE COCHRAN	21 years 6 months	Car crash
SID VICIOUS (Sex Pistols)	21 years 8 months	Drug related
BUDDY HOLLY	22 years 5 months	Plane crash
BOBBY FULLER (Bobby Fuller Four)	22 years 8 months	Murdered
MEL APPLEBY (Mel & Kim)	23 years 6 months	Cancer
JOHNNY ACE (Top R&B act)	25 years 5 months	Russian roulette
FRANKIE LYMON	25 years 7 months	Drug related
PAUL KOSSOF (Free)	25 years 6 months	Drug related
DUANE ALLMAN (Allman Brothers)	25 years 9 months	Bike crash
OTIS REDDING	26 years 3 months	Plane crash
JOHNNY KIDD (Johnny Kidd & The Pirates)	26 years 9 months	Car crash
GRAM PARSONS (Byrds, Flying Burrito Brothers)	26 years 10 months	Drug related
BRIAN JONES (Rolling Stones)	27 years 4 months	Drowned
JIM MORRISON (Doors)	27 years 5 months	Drug related
JANIS JOPLIN	27 years 8 months	Drug related
JIMI HENDRIX	27 years 9 months	Drug related
PETE HAMM (Badfinger)	27 years 11 months	Suicide
JESSE BELVIN (R&B act)	28 years 1 month	Car crash
LINDA JONES (R&B act)	28 years 2 months	Diabetes

ACT	AGE DIED	CAUSE OF DEATH
SHORTY LONG (R&B act)	29 years 1 month	Drowned
HANK WILLIAMS	29 years 3 months	Heart attack
BIG BOPPER	29 years 4 months	Plane crash
ANDY GIBB	30 years 0 months	Drug related
MARC BOLAN	30 years 2 months	Car crash
CHUCK WILLIS (Top R&B act)	30 years 2 months	Peritonitis
PATSY CLINE (Top country act)	30 years 5 months	Plane crash
LITTLE WILLIE JOHN (Top R&B act)	30 years 6 months	Heart attack (in prison)
JOHNNY BURNETTE	30 years 9 months	Drowned
JIM CROCE	30 years 8 months	Plane crash
THOMAS WAYNE (US R 'n' R/pop act)	31 years 0 months	Car crash
JOHN ROSTILL (Shadows)	31 years 5 months	Electrocuted
MINNIE RIPPERTON	31 years 8 months	Cancer
KEITH MOON (Who)	32 years 0 months	Drink related
JON BONHAM (Led Zeppelin)	32 years 3 months	Drink related
FLORENCE BALLARD (Supremes)	32 years 7 months	Heart attack
BILLY STEWART (Top R&B act)	32 years 9 months	Car crash
SHIRLEY BRICKLEY (Orlons)	32 years 10 months	Shot
MAMA CASS ELLIOT	32 years 10 months	Heart attack
KAREN CARPENTER	32 years 11 months	Heart attack
KEITH RELF (Yardbirds)	33 years 1 month	Electrocuted
JOHN BELUSHI (Blues Brothers)	33 years 1 month	Drug related
DONNY HATHAWAY	33 years 3 months	Supposed suicide
DINO MARTIN (Dino, Desi & Billy)	33 years 4 months	Plane crash
JOHNNY HORTON (Top country act)	33 years 6 months	Car crash
BON SCOTT (AC/DC)	33 years 7 months	Drink related
SAM COOKE	33 years 9 months	Shot
KEITH WHITLEY (Top country act)	33 years 10 months	Drink related
PAUL WILLIAMS (Temptations)	34 years 1 month	Suicide
LOWELL GEORGE (Little Feat)	34 years 2 months	Drug related
PHIL LYNOTT (Thin Lizzy)	34 years 4 months	Drug related
ALMA COGAN (Top UK pop/MOR act)	34 years 5 months	Cancer

FINAL VINYL

♦ The aptly titled last Top 40 hit from 60s star **Bobby Rydell** was 'Forget Him' in 1963, and 20 years later **Billy Fury** made his last UK chart appearance with a different song by the same title. Consistent 70s hitmakers the **Darts** appeared in the Top 20 for the last time in 1980 with 'Let's Hang On' and **Roger Whittaker** ended his run of UK hit singles with 'The Last Farewell' in 1975. It's also worth mentioning that the last Top 20 hit from **Bucks Fizz** was called 'New Beginning' (1986) and from top US group **Shalamar** it was 'Disappearing Act' (1983)!

♦ The first posthumous release from **Buddy Holly** was 'It Doesn't Matter Anymore' whilst **Jim Reeves**' was 'I Won't Forget You', **Eddie Cochran**'s was 'Three Steps To Heaven' and **Elvis Presley**'s was 'Way Down'. Stranger still is the fact that country superstar **Hank Williams**' last hit single before he died was 'I'll Never Get Out Of This World Alive' and 50s R&B star **Chuck Willis**' last before he passed on was 'What Am I Living For' coupled with 'Hang Up My Rock 'n' Roll Shoes'.

♦ The record for the most successful chart week by a posthumous act in the US is held, not by **Elvis** or **John Lennon**, but by the late **Jim Croce**, who on 26th January, 1974, held the top two places on the US LP chart and

Eddie Cochran, *who recorded 'Three Steps To Heaven' just weeks before he died.*

had another album at no. 20. He also had three singles on the Top 100 and a Top 10 on the Easy Listening chart.

♦ As a rule, when an artist dies America's memory, at least in chart terms, is shorter than the UK's where acts like **Elvis Presley**, **Buddy Holly** (he featured in the Top 10 LPs 30 years after his death), **Eddie Cochran**, **Jim Reeves**, **Jackie Wilson**, **John Lennon** and **Marc Bolan** continued to chart long after their sad demise. Occasionally, other acts such as **Sam Cooke**, **Nat 'King' Cole**, **Patsy Cline** and **Laurel & Hardy** scored hits (sometimes their first) many years after they had died. One of the rarer posthumous US hits occurred in 1988 when **Louis Armstrong**, who had first charted in 1926, made the Top 40 with 'What A Wonderful World', a song he had taken to the top in the UK 20 years earlier. Louis incidentally, had died some 17 years earlier in 1971, which was before one of his fellow chart acts in 1988 – **Tiffany** – was even born!

♦ The fastest moving single on the US country chart in the last 20 years has been **Red Sovine**'s 'Teddy Bear', which hit the top after just five weeks on the chart in 1976. In Britain it took a little longer to reach its peak of no. 4, namely five years from its 1976 release to 1981 – a year after the singer had passed away.

♦ During the week of the tragic air crash which killed **Buddy Holly**, **Ritchie Valens** and the **Big Bopper** (3rd February, 1959), only Buddy did not have one of his songs in the UK Top 20. Ritchie's 'Come On Let's Go' was there (as recorded by **Tommy**

Steele) and the Big Bopper was there with his song 'Chantilly Lace'. This probably explains the reason that the Big Bopper had top billing over Buddy in the UK national press in stories about the fatal crash. Incidentally, on the morning after the crash a legal letter arrived for Buddy telling him he could no longer use the word **Crickets** in his backing group's name.

♦ The late **Roy Orbison** never had any major US album successes in his lifetime, but after his death in 1989 he held the top two places on the US CD chart with his *Mystery Girl* and with eponymous *Traveling Wilburys* – the super-group that he was part of. These same two LPs also held the top two rungs on the Canadian and Australian pop charts.

♦ Shortly after his death in 1988, **Roy Orbison**'s estate was sued for $1 million by his music publishers for not honouring the five-year deal he signed with them in 1985.

♦ In March, 1990, a few months before his untimely death, **Stevie Ray Vaughan** was voted Musician of the Decade in the Austin (Texas) Music Awards.

♦ The late **Keith Moon**, at one time the drummer with **The Who**, died after watching the film of the **Buddy Holly** story on the anniversary of Buddy's birth. Also, top producer and big fan of Buddy's, **Joe Meek**, died on the anniversary of Buddy's death in 1967. Incidentally, Keith died in the flat that **Mama Cass** had previously died in – it was owned by **Nilsson**, whose biggest hit, the suicidal 'Without You', was written by **Peter Hamm** and **Tom Evans**, who sadly both committed suicide.

*'Way Down' shot way up after the news of **Elvis**' untimely death.*

♦ It's interesting how the death of an artist seems to create an instant demand for their latest releases, even when the record is dropping down the chart or is coming to a halt. For instance, **Elvis Presley**'s 'Way Down' crawled up only four places from 46 to 42 on the UK chart the week before his death and then leaped to no. 4 seven days later. Similarly, **John Lennon**'s single when he was murdered – '(Just Like) Starting Over' – had peaked at no. 8 and was already out of the Top 20 in the UK when news of his death produced an immediate leap to no. 1, where it was followed in the next two months by two more of his records 'Happy Xmas (War Is Over)' and 'Imagine'. John's *Double Fantasy* album, which had peaked at no. 14 and was dropping also sped to the top. Looking further back, **Buddy Holly**'s last single before his death, 'Heartbeat', stalled at no. 30 in the UK and his last single with the **Crickets** did not chart on either side of the Atlantic. However, his first posthumous release, 'It Doesn't Matter Anymore', shot to no. 1 in the UK and returned him to the US Top 20 for the first time in 16 months.

WE DIDN'T START THE FIRE

THIS IS MY SONG

♦ Not every chart-topping song was written by, or especially for, the singer who took it to the top.

As the list below shows, many were written by other artists who, for one reason or another, did not score a hit with it themselves.

THIS IS MY SONG – NO. 1s WRITTEN BY OTHER ARTISTS

YEAR	TITLE	SONGWRITER (NO. 1 SINGER)
1956	'Sixteen Tons'	Merle Travis (Tennessee Ernie Ford)
1956	'Memories Are Made Of This'	Terry Gilkyson (Dean Martin)
1957	'Gamblin' Man'	Woody Guthrie (Lonnie Donegan)
1958	'Claudette'	Roy Orbison (Everly Brothers)
1958	'When'	Paul Evans (Kalin Twins)
1958	'Stupid Cupid'	Neil Sedaka (Connie Francis)
1959	'It Doesn't Matter Anymore'	Paul Anka (Buddy Holly)
1960	'Running Bear'	Big Bopper (Johnny Preston)
1961	'Walk Right Back'	Sonny Curtis (Everly Brothers)
1961	'Wooden Heart'	Bert Kaempfert (Elvis Presley)
1962	'I Can't Stop Loving You'	Don Gibson (Ray Charles)
1963	'Dance On'	Avons (Shadows)
1964	'World Without Love'	Beatles (Peter & Gordon)
1965	'Mr. Tambourine Man'	Bob Dylan (Byrds)
1966	'Michelle'	Beatles (Overlanders)
1966	'Strangers In The Night'	Bert Kaempfert (Frank Sinatra)
1966	'Out Of Time'	Rolling Stones (Chris Farlowe)
1967	'I'm A Believer'	John Stewart (Monkees)
1967	'This Is My Song'	Charlie Chaplin (Petula Clark)
1967	'San Francisco'	John Phillips (Scott McKenzie)
1968	'Mighty Quinn'	Bob Dylan (Manfred Mann)
1968	'With A Little Help From My Friends'	Beatles (Joe Cocker/Wet Wet Wet)
1969	'Ob-la-di Ob-la-da'	Beatles (Marmalade)
1969	'Sugar Sugar'	Andy Kim (Archies)
1972	'Without You'	Ham & Evans of Badfinger (Nilsson)
1973	'The Puppy Song'	Nilsson (David Cassidy)
1974	'Seasons In The Sun'	Rod McKuen (Terry Jacks)
1974	'Love Me For A Reason'	Johnny Bristol (Osmonds)

YEAR	TITLE	SONGWRITER (NO. 1 SINGER)
1974	'Sad Sweet Dreamer'	David Parton (Sweet Sensation)
1979	'Bright Eyes'	Mike Batt (Art Garfunkel)
1979	'Ring My Bell'	Frederick Knight (Anita Ward)
1979	'One Day At A Time'	Kris Kristofferson (Lena Martell)
1980	'Crying'	Roy Orbison (Don McLean)
1980	'Feels Like I'm In Love'	Ray Dorset of Mungo Jerry (Kelly Marie)
1980	'Woman In Love'	Bee Gees (Barbra Streisand)
1980	'The Tide Is High'	John Holt (Blondie)
1981	'Jealous Guy'	John Lennon (Roxy Music)
1983	'Only You'	Vince Clarke (Flying Pickets)
1985	'A Good Heart'	Maria McKee (Feargal Sharkey)
1986	'Chain Reaction'	Bee Gees (Diana Ross)
1987	'I Knew You Were Waiting (For Me)'	Simon Climie (Aretha Franklin & George Michael)
1987	'Nothing's Gonna Stop Us Now'	Albert Hammond (Starship)
1987	'I Wanna Dance With Somebody'	Boy Meets Girl (Whitney Houston)
1988	'One Moment In Time'	Albert Hammond (Whitney Houston)

UNDERCOVER

♦ In the 1950s **'cover versions'** were commonplace on both sides of the Atlantic. This is of course the practice of an artist (usually a well known one) recording or copying an existing record already by another act (usually an unknown or lesser known one). Nowadays, this sort of thing seldom happens but in the past some artists made lucrative careers from copying other people's work. One of the worst offenders was **Pat Boone**, who had over a dozen hits with covers and who, in January, 1956, had four covers on the US Top 100 simultaneously. Other acts who often hit at the expense of others in the US include the **Diamonds**, the **Crew Cuts**, **Georgia Gibbs**, the **Fontaine Sisters** and **Gale Storm**. Don't imagine though that British artists were above this practice – quite the opposite! It was the normal thing for every major US hit by an act unknown in Britain to be covered by an artist who could promote the record live and steal the chart honours. Amongst the British cover 'giants' in the 50s were **Craig Douglas**, **Marty Wilde** and **Frankie Vaughan**. There were, however, scores more.

♦ British covers and similarly uncreative revivals (ie the record was not a brand new release) continued at a great pace in the Swingin' (or should that be the Stealin') 60s. In fact, further investigation reveals that many of the songs which gave British acts hits on both sides of the Atlantic had originally been recorded by American acts (usually little known and often black). Nearly all the major acts of the period were guilty of this practice, including the **Beatles**, the **Rolling Stones**, the **Hollies**, **Moody Blues** and **Manfred Mann**. Among the worst offenders of the 50s and 60s were **Craig Douglas** and the **Searchers** whose chart successes

*The **Rolling Stones** who gained satisfaction by covering American songs.*

included the following cover
versions:

CRAIG DOUGLAS (hits between 1959–62)

TITLE	ORIGINAL RECORDING ARTISTS
'A TEENAGER IN LOVE'	DION & THE BELMONTS
'ONLY SIXTEEN'	SAM COOKE
'PRETTY BLUE EYES'	STEVE LAWRENCE
'A HUNDRED POUNDS OF CLAY'	GENE McDANIELS
'TIME'	JERRY JACKSON
'WHEN MY LITTLE GIRL IS SMILING'	DRIFTERS
'OUR FAVOURITE MELODIES'	GARY CRISS
'OH LONESOME ME'	DON GIBSON

SEARCHERS (hits between 1963–65)

TITLE	ORIGINAL RECORDING ARTISTS
'SWEETS FOR MY SWEET'	DRIFTERS
'SWEET NOTHINS'	BRENDA LEE
'NEEDLES AND PINS'	JACKIE DE SHANNON
'DON'T THROW YOUR LOVE AWAY'	ORLONS
'SOMEDAY WE'RE GONNA LOVE AGAIN'	BARBARA LEWIS
'WHEN YOU WALK IN THE ROOM'	JACKIE DE SHANNON
'GOODBYE MY LOVE'	JIMMY HUGHES

♦ The first time a **Beatles'**
release was covered was in the US
in 1962, when top instrumental
group the **Ventures** released
their version of the oldie 'My
Bonnie' a week after the **Beat**

Brothers (as the Fab Four were then called) version came out Stateside – which was, of course, before they had even made the British chart! The group were one of three British acts the Ventures covered on singles in the early 60s, the others being the **Shadows** ('The Stranger') and **Dakotas** ('The Cruel Sea') – all three original and cover records were US flops. Incidentally, the Ventures released an LP, *Telstar*, in direct competition to the **Tornados** album and outsold the British group who had had the US no. 1 single with the title track.

THE SECOND TIME AROUND

♦ It is not uncommon for a song to resurface some years after it was originally on the chart – often a new recording of it will send it zooming up the hit parade. The following is a list of those songs which, when re-recorded, went right to the top in the UK.

ORIGINAL VERSIONS OF UK NO. 1s FROM THE LAST 25 YEARS

TITLE	ORIGINAL VERSION	NO. 1 COVER (YEAR)
'Unchained Melody'	Todd Duncan	Righteous Brothers (1990)
'Itsy Bitsy Teeny Weeny ...'	Brian Hyland	Bombalarina (1990)
'Dub (Just) Be Good To Me'	S.O.S. Band	Beats International (1990)
'Nothing Comapres 2 U'	Family	Sinead O'Connor (1990)
'Tears On My Pillow'	Little Anthony	Kylie Minogue (1990)
'Sealed With A Kiss'	Brian Hyland	Jason Donovan (1990)
'Ferry Cross The Mersey'	Gerry & The Pacemakers	Marsden/McCartney/Johnson/ Christians (1989)
'Something's Gotten Hold Of My Heart'	Gene Pitney	Marc Almond/Gene Pitney (1989)
'A Groovy Kind Of Love'	Patti Labelle & Bluebells	Phil Collins (1988)
'The Only Way Is Up'	Otis Clay	Yazz (1988)
'Nothing's Gonna Change My Love For You'	George Benson	Glenn Medeiros (1988)
'Don't Turn Around'	Tina Turner	Aswad (1988)
'I Think We're Alone Now'	Tommy James & Shondells	Tiffany (1988)
'Always On My Mind'	Brenda Lee	Pet Shop Boys (1987)
'La Bamba'	Ritchie Valens	Los Lobos (1987)
'Everything I Own'	Bread	Boy George (1987)/ Ken Boothe (1974)
'Caravan Of Love'	Isley, Jasper & Isley	Housemartins (1986)
'I Want To Wake Up With You'	Mac Davis	Boris Gardiner (1986)
'Saving All My Love For You'	McCoo & Davis	Whitney Houston (1985)
'I Feel For You'	Prince	Chaka Khan (1984)
'Red Red Wine'	Neil Diamond	UB40 (1983)
'Wherever I Lay My Hat'	Marvin Gaye	Paul Young (1983)
'Pass The Dutchie'	Mighty Diamonds	Musical Youth (1982)
'Tainted Love'	Gloria Jones	Soft Cell (1981)
'Together We Are Beautiful'	Ken Leray	Fern Kinney (1980)
'One Day At A Time'	Marilyn Sellars	Lena Martell (1979)
'Mary's Boy Child'	Harry Belafonte	Boney M (1978)

TITLE	ORIGINAL VERSION	NO. 1 COVER (YEAR)
'Rivers Of Babylon'	Melodians	Boney M (1978)
'I Don't Want To Talk About It'	Crazy Horse	Rod Stewart (1977)
'Chanson D'Amour'	Art & Dotty Todd	Manhattan Transfer (1977)
'Under The Moon Of Love'	Curtis Lee	Showaddywaddy (1976)
'No Charge'	Melba Montgomery	J.J. Barrie (1976)
'Sailing'	Sutherland Brothers	Rod Stewart (1975)
'Oh Boy'	Crickets	Mud (1975)
'Bye Bye Baby'	Four Seasons	Bay City Rollers (1975)
'If'	Bread	Telly Savalas (1975)
'Young Love'	Ric Cartey	Donny Osmond (1973)/ Tab Hunter (1957)
'The Twelfth Of Never'	Johnny Mathis	Donny Osmond (1973)
'How Can I Be Sure'	Young Rascals	David Cassidy (1972)
'Puppy Love'	Paul Anka	Donny Osmond (1972)
'Son Of My Father'	Georgio Moroder	Chicory Tip (1972)
'Chirpy Chirpy Cheep Cheep'	Lally Stott	Middle Of The Road (1971)
'I Hear You Knockin''	Smiley Lewis	Dave Edmunds (1970)
'Woodstock'	Joni Mitchell	Matthews' Southern Comfort (1970)
'The Wonder Of You'	Ray Peterson	Elvis Presley (1970)
'I Heard It Through The Grapevine'	Gladys Knight	Marvin Gaye (1969)
'Cinderella Rockefella'	Mason Williams	Esther & Abi Ofarim (1968)
'Those Were The Days'	Limeliters	Mary Hopkin (1968)
'Everlasting Love'	Robert Knight	Love Affair (1968)
'Silence Is Golden'	Four Seasons	Tremeloes (1967)
'Release Me'	Jimmy Dean	Engelbert Humperdinck (1967)
'Green Green Grass Of Home'	Johnny Darrell	Tom Jones (1966)
'The Sun Ain't Gonna Shine Anymore'	Frankie Valli	Walker Brothers (1966)

GOING FOR A SONG

♦ **Lionel Richie** broke a songwriting record when he became the first writer to pen a US no. 1 single for nine consecutive years (1978–1986). The songs concerned were 'Three Times A Lady' (78), 'Still' (79) both recorded by the **Commodores**, 'Lady' (80) sung by **Kenny Rogers**, 'Endless Love' (81) which Lionel sang with **Diana Ross**, four of his solo hits 'Truly' (82), 'All Night Long' (83), 'Hello' and 'Say You Say Me' (86),

'Three Times A Lady' was one of the songs that made **Lionel Richie** *nine times a chart-topper.*

and 'We Are The World' by **USA For Africa** which he sang on.

♦ Only **Irving Berlin** has written more no. 1s than **Lionel Richie**, nine in total, but they were not in consecutive years. Also, Lionel is the only person to have produced the US no. 1 pop, soul and country records in the same week. The records were: 'Endless Love', his duet with **Diana Ross** which headed the pop and soul charts and 'I Don't Need You' by **Kenny Rogers** which was the country chart topper on 15th August, 1981.

♦ Probably the least heralded songwriter to have written the top two songs on the US chart in any one week was **Kenny Nolan** whose compositions 'My Eyes Adored You', recorded by **Frankie Valli** and 'Lady Marmalade', recorded by **Labelle**, held those two spots in 1975. As a singer Kenny's biggest success was the US no. 3 hit 'I Like Dreamin'' in 1976. He was also in the group **Eleventh Hour** who originally recorded the controversial 'Lady Marmalade'.

♦ Other little known but highly successful writers include the duo **Billy Steinberg** and **Tom Kelly**, who wrote five US no. 1s in five years. Their songs were: 'Like A Virgin' (**Madonna**) in 1984, 'True Colors' (**Cyndi Lauper**) in 1986, 'Alone' (**Heart**) in 1987, 'So Emotional' (**Whitney Houston**) in 1988 and 'Eternal Flame' (**Bangles**) in 1989.

♦ In Britain, apart from the songwriting teams of **Stock Aitken Waterman** and **Lennon & McCartney**, who have both written consecutive no. 1s on three separate occasions, the only other people who have written consecutive chart-toppers are:

Burt Bacharach & Hal David who did it in 1958 with 'The Story Of My Life' (Michael Holliday) and 'Magic Moments' (Perry Como).

Bruce Welch who co-wrote 'Summer Holiday' (Cliff Richard) and 'Foot Tapper' (Shadows) in 1963.

Tony Macaulay & John McLeod who in 1967 wrote 'Baby Now That I Found You' (Foundations) and 'Let The Heartaches Begin' (Long John Baldry).

Nicky Chinn & Mike Chapman who composed Mud's 'Tiger Feet' and Suzi Quatro's 'Devil Gate Drive' in 1974.

John Lennon who on his own wrote the two 1981 chart toppers 'Imagine' and 'Woman'.

♦ The most successful non-performing female songwriter of all time is **Diane Warren**, who has seen 13 of her songs go into the US Top 10 since 1987. In October, 1989, she had five of her songs recorded by five different acts climbing the US Top 100 and a couple of weeks later she became the first non-performing female writer to write America's top two singles which were 'When I See You Smile', recorded by **Bad English**, and 'Blame It On The Rain' by **Milli Vanilli**.

♦ Songwriter **Michael Carr**, who composed the **Shadows'** British smashes 'Kon-Tiki' and 'Man Of Mystery' in the 60s, also wrote the war-time favourite 'We're Gonna Hang Out The Washing On The Siegfried Line'.

♦ Sheffield (England) born musician and composer **Rod Temperton** (who is white) has written four US no. 1s performed by black American artists. The songs are 'Rock With You' by

Michael Jackson, 'Stomp' by **Brothers Johnson**, 'Give Me The Night' by **George Benson** and 'Baby Come To Me' by **Patti Austin and James Ingram**. This ex-member of **Heatwave** also wrote such classic dance hits as 'Thriller', 'Boogie Nights', 'Always And Forever', 'Off The Wall' and 'Sweet Freedom'.

♦ **Paul Anka**, the first white teenager to top the UK charts, had three of his compositions simultaneously on the US country chart 21 years after his debut single 'Diana' (which was a transatlantic chart-topper for him before his 16th birthday). The songs were 'I Do Love You', 'My Way' and 'It Doesn't Matter Anymore', which were hits by **Donna Fargo**, **Elvis Presley** and **R.C. Bannon** respectively.

♦ The first black female artist to write a UK no. 1 hit was **Phyllis Nelson**, who in 1985 wrote and sang 'Move Closer'. Incidentally, the record, which in the midst of the video age had no video, did not even make the US chart. However, the follow-up 'I Like You' did not chart in the UK yet topped the dance charts in her native America.

♦ American songwriter **Bob Merrill** had a record 26 big UK hits in the 50s, including '(How Much Is That) Doggie In The Window', 'Mambo Italiano', 'Feet Up', 'Sweet Old Fashioned Girl', 'Sparrow In The Treetop' and 'If I Knew You Were Comin' I'd 've Baked A Cake'.

♦ **Dan Hartman**, who had Top 10 hits like 'Instant Replay' in 1978, and 'I Can Dream About It' in 1984, had two UK Top 5 entries in September, 1989 – his composition 'Ride On Time' by Black Box and his production 'The

Best' by Tina Turner. In 1990, the now defunct duo **Yell!** hit the no. 10 spot with their version of his 'Instant Replay'.

♦ The only song to be in the UK Top 20 with four separate versions simultaneously is 'Unchained Melody'. This occurred in 1955 and the versions were by **Al Hibbler**, **Jimmy Young**, **Les Baxter** and **Liberace**. Strangely enough, there were two versions of this song together in the US Top 20 in 1990 and both were by the same act – the **Righteous Brothers**. One recorded in 1965 and the other 25 years later. Incidentally, when the Righteous Brothers' hit the top with the song in the UK in 1990, it broke the record for the longest gap between no. 1 hits for an artist, coming 25 years after their last chart-topper 'You've Lost That Lovin' Feeling'.

♦ Up until October, 1989, ten different songs with the title 'Hold On' had charted in the US – the artists being **Santana**, **Ian Gomm**, **Triumph**, **Kansas**, **Sons of Champlin**, **Rascals**, **Badfinger**, **Wild Cherry**, the **Radiants** and **Donny Osmond**. Amazingly, every one of them failed to chart in Britain. However, in 1990 two more songs by that name hit in the US and oddly both also became big UK hits – they were by the all-female groups **En Vogue** and **Wilson Phillips**.

♦ The most charted title in the UK is 'Tonight' with ten different songs of that name scoring a hit. The acts who charted with it were: **Shirley Bassey** (1962), **Move** (1971), **Rubettes** (1974), **Zaine Griff** (1980), **Modettes** (1981), **Steve Harvey** (1983), **David Bowie**, **Kool & The Gang**

The Goss twins, **Bros**, *scored a Christmas cracker in 1988.*

and **Boomtown Rats** (1984) and **New Kids On The Block** (1990).

♦ In America, the first song to chart in each of the six decades that the official singles chart has existed was 'In The Mood'. In the 1940s **Glenn Miller** had the hit, in the 50s it was **Johnny Maddox** and in the 60s **Ernie Fields**. In the 70s **Bette Midler** and the **Henhouse Five Plus Two** (a pseudonym for **Ray Stevens**) both scored with the song. In the 80s it was included on 'Hooked On Big Bands' by **Frank Barber**. In 1990, the song appeared on the UK hit 'Let's Swing The Mood' by **Jive Bunny & The Mastermixers**.

♦ The song with the longest chart span on the UK chart was written on Christmas Eve, 1818. It is the Christmas favourite 'Silent Night' which, recorded by **Bing Crosby**, hit a month after UK charts started in 1952 and was back on the charts, in **Bros'** version, in 1988.

♦ Two big US rock 'n' roll hit songs of the 50s, 'To Know Him Is To Love Him' and 'In The Still Of The Night' both won awards for being the top country song of the year in the 80s. The former song

was originally a hit for its composer, **Phil Spector**, and his group the **Teddy Bears** in 1958 and was a country no. 1 for **Dolly Parton, Linda Ronstadt & Emmylou Harris** in 1987. The latter song, which was never a UK hit, is known as New York's favourite oldie and the original version by the **Five Satins** from 1956 also appeared on the four-million-selling album *Dirty Dancing*. It hit the top of the country chart as part of 'Lost In The 50s Tonight' by **Ronnie Milsap** in 1985.

♦ The London pub song 'Down At The Old Bull And Bush', which was often sung to raise morale during the World Wars, was originally a German drinking song called 'Under The Anheuser Bush'.

♦ The song 'Little Bitty Pretty One' has been a US hit for its composer **Bobby Day**, as well as for **Thurston Harris, Frankie Lymon** and **Clyde McPhatter**, all of whom have since died. The only living act to have charted with the song are the **Jackson Five**.

♦ In September, 1978, the **Jacksons** and a certain **Michael Jackson** had a chart battle over the same song – 'Blame It On The Boogie'. The song, written by Michael, became a hit for the group on both sides of the Atlantic. Its British composer Michael, who recorded it as **Mick Jackson**, also had a transatlantic hit with the song. Mick, by the way, fronted his own band who happened to be called **Jacko**!

♦ Strangely, those classic Irish songs 'When Irish Eyes Are Smiling' and 'Mother McRee' were both written in Ohio and those famous British standard songs 'Goodbye Dolly Gray' and 'Nellie Dean' are also both American-written songs.

♦ If you have ever wondered why a song about a maniac should appear in a film like *Flashdance*, it

may interest you to know that the US no. 1 hit 'Maniac' by **Michael Sembello** was actually written for a horror film and was sent to the producers of *Flashdance* for possible inclusion by mistake!

♦ The first song to enter the UK chart (sheet music only at the time) at no. 1 was 'Galway Bay', in 1948. Amongst the popular versions of the song were those by **Bing Crosby**, **Anne Shelton**, **Joe Loss** and **Josef Locke**.

♦ Quite often, a hit song starts its life under a different title – the best known example being the **Beatles**' 'Yesterday' which first saw the light of day as 'Scrambled Eggs'. Amongst the many other songs that started life as something else are:

ORIGINAL TITLE	HIT TITLE, ARTIST
'CINDY LOU'	'PEGGY SUE' – BUDDY HOLLY
'EUROPEAN QUEEN'	'CARIBBEAN QUEEN' – BILLY OCEAN
'FOR JOHN AND PAUL'	'SUNSHINE SUPERMAN' – DONOVAN
'GREAT TO BE YOUNG'	'TEENAGER IN LOVE' – DION/MARTY WILDE
'GYPSIES AND WHITE TRASH'	'GYPSIES TRAMPS & THIEVES' – CHER
'HEY MISTER'	'THE MOST BEAUTIFUL GIRL IN THE WORLD' – CHARLIE RICH
'I'LL BE TRUE TO YOU'	'SOLDIER BOY' – SHIRELLES
'I'LL BE TRUE TO YOU'	'YES I WILL' – HOLLIES
'JENNY'	'STRANGER ON THE SHORE' – ACKER BILK
'K.C. LOVIN''	'KANSAS CITY' – WILBERT HARRISON
'LIVERPOOL SUNSET'	'WATERLOO SUNSET' – KINKS
'RUN RABBIT RUN'	'FLY ROBIN FLY' – SILVER CONVENTION
'69 TEARS'	'96 TEARS' – ? & THE MYSTERIANS/ STRANGLERS
'STILETTO'	'WIPEOUT' – SURFARIS/FAT BOYS
'TELL THE WORLD'	'WHEELS' – STRING-A-LONGS
'TWINKLE'	'LONELY BULL' – TIJUANA BRASS
'UE O MUITE ARUKO'	'SUKIYAKI' – KYU SAKAMOTO
'WHY DO BIRDS SING SO GAY'	'WHY DO FOOLS FALL IN LOVE' – TEENAGERS/DIANA ROSS
'WOP BOP A LOO BOP'	'TUTTI FRUTTI' – LITTLE RICHARD

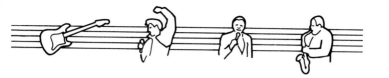

STARMAKER

FIRST RELEASES

◆ The first single releases from a selection of interesting and important record labels in the US and UK.

LABEL	ARTIST	TITLE	YEAR
A&M (US)	HERB ALPERT	'THE LONELY BULL'	1962
APPLE (UK)	BEATLES	'HEY JUDE'	1968
ARISTA (US)	ROBBY BENSON	'A ROCK AND ROLL SONG'	1975
ASYLUM (US)	JUDEE SILL	'JESUS WAS A CROSS MAKER'	1972
ATCO (US)	PAULINE ROGERS	'UP TILL NOW'	1955
ATLANTIC (US)	EDDIE SAFRANSKI	'SAFRANTIC'	1948
ATLANTIC (UK)	DRIFTERS	'UNDER THE BOARDWALK'	1964
BELL (US)	EGGHEADS	'FOOLIN' AROUND'	1964
BELL (UK)	BOX TOPS	'CRY LIKE A BABY'	1968
CAPITOL (US)	PAUL WHITEMAN	'I FOUND A NEW BABY'	1942
CREATION (UK)	THE LEGEND!	'73 IN '83'	1983
DERAM (UK)	BEVERLY	'HAPPY NEW YEAR'	1966
ELEKTRA (US)	DIAN & GREENBRIAR BOYS	'BROWNS FERRY BLUES'	1963
EMI (UK)	REAL THING	'PLASTIC MAN'	1973
EPIC (US)	BROTHER LEE ROY BAND	'MAN ON THE BEAT'	1953
FACTORY (UK)	VARIOUS	'A FACTORY SAMPLE' (EP)	1979
FONTANA (UK)	JIMMY JAQUES	'COME WALKING'	1958
4AD (UK)	FAST SET	'JUNCTION ONE'	1980
GEFFEN (US)	DONNA SUMMER	'THE WANDERER'	1980
IMMEDIATE (UK)	McCOYS	'HANG ON SLOOPY'	1965
LONDON (UK)	AL MORGAN	'JEALOUS HEART'	1949
MCA (US)	ELTON JOHN	'CROCODILE ROCK'	1972
MCA (UK)	JOHN ROWLES	'IF I ONLY HAD TIME'	1968
MERCURY (UK)	RUSTY DRAPER	'ARE YOU SATISFIED'	1956
MOTOWN (US)	SATINTONES	'MY BELOVED'	1961
PHILIPS (UK)	JOHNNY BRANDON	'THE GLOW WORM'	1953
POLYDOR (UK)	CATERINA VALENTE	'MY LONELY LOVER'	1955
PRIVATE STOCK (US)	ARROWS	'TOUCH TOO MUCH'	1974
PRIVATE STOCK (UK)	FRANKIE VALLI	'MY EYES ADORED YOU'	1974
PWL (UK)	MANDY SMITH	'I JUST CAN'T WAIT'	1987
PYE INTERNATIONAL	RITCHIE VALENS	'COME ON LET'S GO'	1958
REPRISE (US)	FRANK SINATRA	'THE SECOND TIME AROUND'	1961

LABEL	ARTIST	TITLE	YEAR
RHYTHM KING (UK)	Q-PID WITH NIKKI D	'MY LATIN LOVER'	1986
ROUGH TRADE (UK)	METAL URBAIN	'PARIS MARQUIS'	1978
SIRE (US)	ERIC MARSHALL	'I CAN'T LOVE YOU ANYMORE'	1968
SIRE (UK)	REZILLOS	'TOP OF THE POPS'	1978
STATESIDE (UK)	FREDDY CANNON	'PALISADES PARK'	1962
STAX (US)	VEL-TONES	'SOMEDAY'	1959
STIFF (UK)	NICK LOWE	'SO IT GOES'	1976
TAMLA (US)	MARV JOHNSON	'COME TO ME'	1959
TAMLA MOTOWN (UK)	SUPREMES	'STOP! IN THE NAME OF LOVE'	1965
2 TONE (UK)	SPECIALS	'GANGSTERS'	1979
UA (US)	JOE VALINO	'DECLARATION OF LOVE'	1957
WARNER (US)	SMART SET	'I ONLY HAVE EYES FOR YOU'	1958
WARNER (UK)	EVERLY BROTHERS	'CATHY'S CLOWN'	1960

THE HITMAKERS

♦ On 4th March, 1978, the **Bee Gees** wrote and produced four of the US Top 5 singles and their label **RSO** had all the top three spots on the chart. An unbeatable record you might think, yet in May, 1978, four songs written by the same group followed each other to the no. 1 position on the US chart. The records were their own 'Stayin' Alive' and 'Night Fever', their brother **Andy Gibb**'s '(Love Is) Thicker Than Water' and 'If I Can't Have You' by **Yvonne Elliman**, the first three

It wouldn't be jive talkin' to say that the **Bee Gees** *were the most successful writing/production team of the late 70s.*

Stock Aitken & Waterman - *Britain's most successful production and writing team of all time.*

of which they also produced. At the same time, the little RSO label scored its sixth consecutive no. 1 – a feat that no label had managed before or has done since. The single 'How Deep Is Your Love' from the Bee Gees and 'Baby Come Back' from **Player** had preceded the above four records to the top spot.

♦ In Britain it's **Stock Aitken & Waterman** who come closest to the Bee Gees record. On 18th March, 1989, the trio had three of their productions in the UK Top 4 singles: **Jason Donovan**'s 'Too Many Broken Hearts', **Bananarama/La Na Nee Nee Noo Noo**'s 'Help' and **Donna Summer**'s 'This Time I Know It's For Real', with the first and last of those tracks coming from their own pens. Six months later they managed six singles in the Top 20 with three of them (**Jason Donovan**'s 'Everyday (I Love You More)', **Big Fun**'s 'Blame It On The Boogie' and **Cliff Richard**'s 'I Just Don't Have The Heart') in the Top 5!

♦ In just five years, over 100 of **Stock Aitken & Waterman**'s productions have charted, with an amazing 52 of those making the UK Top 10. Remarkably, the trio also wrote 75 per cent of the hits.

♦ When it comes to UK record labels stringing no. 1 hits together – **Stock Aitken & Waterman**'s PWL label chalked up three in a row in 1989, to equal the three in a row achieved 24 years earlier by **Decca**. PWL's three were **Kylie Minogue**'s 'Hand On Your Heart', 'Ferry 'Cross The Mersey' (a charity record by various Liverpool artists including **Gerry Marsden** and **Paul McCartney**) and 'Sealed With A Kiss' from **Jason Donovan**. At that time, they also held the first two places on the chart for the second time (they had originally achieved this in April, 1987, when 'Let It Be' by **Ferry Aid** was top and 'Respectable' by **Mel & Kim** was in the runner-up position). Incidentally, the record for consecutive no. 1s by one record label goes to **Philips Records**, who held the top place for 22 weeks in 1956/57 with five different records.

♦ **Pete Waterman**, the front man of the team, formed another label prior to the ultra-successful PWL. It was called **Loose End** and he set it up in 1983 after having had a worldwide smash with 'Pass The Dutchie' by **Musical Youth**. The label had a few releases through the top record company **MCA** but failed to chart any records.

♦ The S.A.W. team were also the first producers to have UK no. 1 hits with ten different artists, which they achieved between 1985 and 1989, and the first to have three of their records enter at no. 1. These singles were: **Ferry Aid**'s 'Let It Be', **Christians/Johnson/ McCartney/Marsden**'s 'Ferry 'Cross The Mersey' and **Jason Donovan**'s 'Sealed With A Kiss'. There are, however, two British producers who have had more UK chart-toppers than S.A.W., namely **Norrie Paramor** (who produced many acts of the early 60s, including **Cliff Richard** and **Helen Shapiro**) and **George Martin** (who produced the Beatles) who have both seen 27 of their productions go to the top.

♦ Other staggering statistics about this tremendous trio include the fact that they had at least one record on the UK Top 75 chart every week from 15th March, 1986, to 20th October, 1990, and that they produced 11 of the 40 biggest sellers in the UK in 1989!

♦ Hot American producer and songwriter **Maurice Starr**'s best time on the US chart occurred in July, 1990, when three of the US Top 4 singles were by acts he discovered, these being **New Kids On The Block**, **Bell**, **Biv Devoe** and **Bobby Brown**. Another of his acts, **Johnny Gill**, stood at no. 10 in the same week.

♦ The hottest US production team of recent years are **L.A.** (Reid) and **Kenny 'Babyface' Edmonds**. Amongst their achievements are having 18 US Top 10 hits in just over two years. They also had five singles simultaneously in the US Top 40 in 1989 – the acts concerned were **Sheena Easton**, the **Boys**, **Karyn White** and **Bobby Brown**. They have also had an unprecedented 19 no. 1 R&B hits since mid-1987, eight of them within just nine months. Surprisingly, they had to wait until November, 1990, for the first no. 1 pop hit with **Whitney Houston**'s 'I'll Be Your Baby Tonight'.

♦ **Jim Steinman** is the only person to have produced the top two singles in America by non-American acts. The records were 'Total Eclispe Of The Heart' (no. 1) by **Bonnie Tyler** from Wales, and 'Making Love Out Of Nothing at All' (no. 2) by **Air Supply** from Australia.

MOTOWN MISSES

♦ Motown is known worldwide as the most successful and distinctive soul/black music label with acts including **Stevie Wonder**, **Diana Ross & The Supremes**, **Four Tops**, **Temptations**, **Martha & The Vandellas** and **Rick James**. However, amongst the skeletons in their cupboard you will find such unexpected singles as:

TITLE	ACT & DESCRIPTION	YEAR
'TALKING TO YOUR PICTURE'	TONY MARTIN (50s MOR ballad singer)	1964
'CHAINED'	PAUL PETERSON (60s US pop teen idol)	1967
'MUCK ARTY PARK'	SOUPY SALES (US slapstick comedian)	1969
'OFF TO DUBLIN IN THE GREEN'	ABBEY TAVERN SINGERS (Trad. Irish song)	1969
'LUNEY TAKE OFF'	CAPTAIN ZAP & THE MOTOWN CUT-UPS (novelty)	1969
'NO TIME AT ALL'	IRENE 'GRANNY' RYAN (from 'Beverly Hillbillies' TV show)	1973
'DAN THE BANJO MAN'	DAN THE BANJO MAN (novelty)	1974
'WHERE WERE YOU GOING WHEN THE SHIP WENT DOWN'	DICKEY & THE POSEIDONS (novelty)	1974
'THOSE OTHER MEN'	ALBERT FINNEY (UK actor)	1977
'THE LAST SONG'	LYNDA CARTER (TV's 'Wonder Woman')	1980

♦ Perhaps not surprisingly, none of the above records charted! It's also worth noting that the following unlikely artists also had records out through Motown: **Pat Boone, Meatloaf, Bobby Darin, Pretty Things, Easybeats, Kiki Dee, Chris Rea, Bruce Willis, Lesley Gore, Bruce Channel, Detroit Wheels, Ronnie Dove, T.G. Sheppard** and **Terry Stafford**.

The **Supremes** *- three of Motown's best known misses.*

The King.

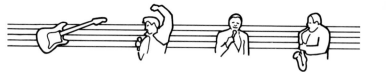

STAR TREKKIN'

ELVIS PRESLEY

♦ Not only did Elvis take the song 'Good Rockin' Tonight' from top 40s R&B singer **Wynonie Harris**' repertoire, but Wynonie also claimed Elvis copied his hip and lip movements. The origins of the King's body gyrations are also claimed by **Bo Diddley** and **Jackie Wilson**, two performers Elvis very much admired.

♦ He was a fan of **James Brown** and often watched his famous performance of 'Please, Please, Please' from the T.A.M.I. show film. He was also a long time fan of R&B group the **Dominoes**, and he told friends he would give anything to sing like the group's original leader **Clyde McPhatter** (he closely copied **McPhatter and the Drifters**' version of 'White Christmas' when he recorded the song in 1957).

♦ He was the first artist to sell ten million records in one year, achieving this feat in 1956. On New Year's Day, 1956, he was unknown to US pop record buyers but before the end of the year he had ten separate tracks on the US Top 100 simultaneously.

♦ The first record in the world to have a million advance orders was his 'Love Me Tender' in 1956, and the first record ever in the UK with over 250 000 advance orders was his 'Jailhouse Rock' in 1958 – which became the first single to enter the chart at no. 1.

♦ On 3rd March, 1960, the King paid his only visit to Britain. En route from Germany to the USA his plane landed for refuelling at Prestwick Airport in Glasgow where he wandered around and talked to some locals and signed autographs whilst waiting for his flight to the States.

♦ No album by a solo performer has spent longer at the top of the UK chart than Elvis' *Blue Hawaii* which had a 17-week residency at no. 1 in 1960. It took 30 years before anyone even came close to his record when **Phil Collins** logged 15 weeks at the top with *. . . But Seriously*.

♦ His 'Return To Sender' (1962) was the last of a record-breaking 24 consecutive US Top 5 singles.

♦ In 1967 the Mid-South Coliseum in Memphis was re-named **The Elvis Presley Coliseum**.

♦ The biggest daily sale ever of an artist's records is claimed to be the 20 million sold worldwide on the day after Elvis' death. Three weeks after his death he had nine singles on the UK chart – oddly though, none of his old tracks returned to the US Top 100. The most staggering chart fact of all is that on 3rd September, 1977 he had 13 LPs in the UK Top 50 and a staggering 27 in the British Top 100 albums!

♦ It is claimed that he has sold over a billion records, which is more than twice the sales of **Bing Crosby** (the runner-up) or the **Beatles**.

CLIFF RICHARD & THE SHADOWS

♦ The act with the most Top 10 single hits in the UK is Cliff Richard with a total of 59 (three in duets). It took him until 1990 to finally steal that record from **Elvis Presley** who had held it for 30 years.

♦ He is also the artist with the most duo hits in Britain – he has hit the Top 20 in duets with **Van Morrison**, **Hank Marvin**, **Sarah Brightman**, **Olivia Newton-John**, **Phil Everly** and with the **Young Ones**. Many of his hits were of course with his group the **Shadows**. He also charted when teamed up with **Elton John** and **Sheila Walsh**, but missed the UK Top 75 when teamed with newcomer **Janet Jackson**, in 1984.

♦ Cliff, not surprisingly, holds the record for appearances on TV's *Top Of The Pops* having been on the show nearly 90 times.

♦ He also holds the record for scoring the most Top 10 albums in the 80s in the UK with 9, which helped push his total world sales up to nearly 80 million.

♦ The Shadows' first recordings, both with and without Cliff, were released under the name the

Drifters which they changed to avoid confusion with the US R&B group of the same name. Oddly though, this change came well after 'Living Doll' had been a US hit (it was listed as 'by **Cliff & The Drifters**' there). However, the name Shadows was already being used by at least one US group (on Del-Fi) and to confuse matters further **Bobby Vee**'s backing group (which once included **Bob Dylan** then known as **Elston Gunn**) were also called the Shadows. Just when things were getting sorted in 1964 along came a successful Irish showband led by **Joe Dolan** called the **Drifters**.

♦ The Shadows were the first British pop act to top the UK LP chart – a feat they achieved six weeks before Cliff, in 1961. They were also the first act to simultaneously top the UK single, EP and LP charts and they were still scoring Top 10 albums in 1990 – a longevity record no other group can match. To date they have had 22 chart albums, though oddly they had to wait until 1989 to have two Top 20 albums in the same year!

Congratulations to bachelor boy **Cliff Richard** – *the most successful British solo artist.*

BEATLES

◆ As the **Silver Beatles** they played a gig with **Gerry & The Pacemakers** at the Grosvenor Ballroom in Wallasey in June, 1960.

◆ They first played at The Cavern club in Liverpool on 21st March, 1961. Their 294th show was their last there, on 3rd August, 1963.

◆ Their first US LP release was *Introducing The Beatles* in July, 1963 – it got nowhere.

◆ The first song they ever sang on TV was 'Some Other Guy', their version of the then recent R&B single by **Richie Barrett** (the man who discovered **Frankie Lymon & The Teenagers** and later managed the **Three Degrees**). The show, screened only in the Granada (North-West England) area, was *People & Places* on 17th October, 1962.

◆ Their first release in the UK was on 5th January, 1962 – it was their version of 'My Bonnie' and the review in the *NME* read: 'The group have above average ideas and a welcome amount of imagination'.

◆ Despite having a small hit with 'Love Me Do' in 1962, the group were not selected by the music press as being 'great possibilities' for 1963 in the annual predictions.

◆ Americans who quickly spotted the group's potential included **Little Richard**, **Tommy Roe** and **Roy Orbison**, who all said they could make it Stateside (Roy also thought **Gerry & The Pacemakers** could be US stars). **Del Shannon** hastily covered 'From Me To You' in 1963 and

*The **Beatles** – a group with 'above average ideas and a welcome amount of imagination'.*

became the first person to chart in the US with a Lennon & McCartney song.

♦ Before they had even charted in the US the group had their best week's showing on the UK charts. It was on 6th December, 1963 that they had no. 1 and 2 on the *NME* chart with 'I Want To Hold Your Hand' and 'She Loves You' and they also had two EPs, 'Twist & Shout' and 'Beatles Hits', and an album *With The Beatles* in the Top 20 singles chart alongside one other song that they had written – 'I Wanna Be Your Man' by the **Rolling Stones**.

♦ They first appeared on US TV on Jack Parr's *Today* show on 3rd January,1964, where film of a UK performance, complete with all the 'Beatlemania' reactions, was shown. A few weeks later they made their first US live TV appearance on Ed Sullivan's show and attracted a record audience of 73 million! Less than two months later their records held the Top 5 spots on the US singles chart.

♦ 'I Want To Hold Your Hand' became the fastest selling single in British history when it sold over a million copies in its first three days of release in 1963, and shortly after it sold 1.8 million in the US in a record five weeks.

♦ The record for simultaneous entries on the US singles chart is 13, which was set in 1964 by the Beatles.

♦ The group's best album chart week in the US came on 2nd May, 1964, when *The Beatles Second Album* was top, *Meet The Beatles* was runner-up and *Introducing The Beatles* stood at no. 4.

♦ **Paul** was presented with the only rhodium record by Guinness to commemorate the fact that he is the world's top-selling songwriter of all time.

♦ Surprisingly, neither of **Paul**'s only two UK no. 1s – 'Mull Of Kintyre' nor 'Pipes Of Peace' made the US Top 100 – which is especially odd when you consider that the former outsold every Beatles single in Britain!

♦ Shortly after his death in 1980, **John Lennon** had a record breaking three UK no. 1 singles in less than two months.

♦ **Paul** has broken numerous records over the years – amongst the lesser known ones is the fact that he is the only songwriter to have had two songs on the US Black Music and Country Music charts simultaneously, which he accomplished in April 1982. The tracks on the Country chart were 'All My Loving' sung by **Mundo Earwood** and 'I've Just Seen A Face' by **Calamity Jane**. The two hits on the Black chart were **Lakeside**'s recording of 'I Want To Hold Your Hand' and 'Ebony And Ivory' by **Paul McCartney and Stevie Wonder**.

♦ Probably the most expensive pop record box set was the complete works of the **Beatles** which included all the solo projects from **John**, **Paul**, **George** and **Ringo**. It was released in Japan in 1982 and sold for £800 ($1250).

♦ The act had the biggest jump ever on the UK LP chart, 17 years after they split up, with their classic LP *Sgt Pepper*, which climbed from no. 97 to no. 3 when it became available on CD for the first time. It was one of 13 UK LP chart entries for the group that year.

♦ They are the only act to hold the Top 4 places on the UK CD chart. They achieved this feat 17 years after they split up on the 14th March, 1987, with *Hard Days Night*, *Please Please Me*, *With The Beatles* and *Beatles For Sale*.

♦ Of course, the group had numerous no. 1 hits with their songs all over the world in the 60s and 70s, but it took until 1989 for a song of theirs to head the country chart. It was 'I Don't Want To Spoil The Party' by **Rosanne Cash**, whose father **Johnny** had been a favourite of the group in the 50s.

♦ It is claimed that **Paul McCartney** holds the record for the number of paid admissions at a one-headline act show when 184 000 people saw him at the Maracana stadium in Brazil, in 1990. Paul also broke the existing record for indoor attendance back in 1976 when 67 000 attended his show in Seattle.

ROLLING STONES

♦ In October, 1963, when reviewing the **Everly Brothers** UK tour the *NME* critic said of the support group 'I can freely admit to bewilderment at recognition of the **Rolling Stones**. They won great appreciation for 'Poison Ivy', 'Fortune Teller', their hit parade success 'Come On' and 'Money'. But not from me.'

♦ The first riot at a Stones concert was said to be at their performance on 24th July, 1964 at the Empress Ballroom in Blackpool.

♦ Their 'Paint It Black' single topped the Dutch charts twice – once in 1966 and again 24 years later, in 1990.

♦ Their first time behind the Iron Curtain was when they played in Warsaw, Poland on 13th April, 1967.

♦ They raised over half a million dollars for the Nicaragua earthquake victims in 1973 from one show at the Forum in Los Angeles.

♦ The Stones made their 1989 US tour debut at Toads Night Club in New Haven, Connecticut. They played a 55-minute set in front of just 700 people.

♦ Of the top 20 grossing individual shows in the US in 1989, the group held an amazing 15 positions (interestingly, another UK act, the **Who**, held three of the remaining five positions). The group earned over a $100 million from this tour – a world record. The 'pay per view' TV coverage of a live show from the tour broke the US record for any similar musical event with over 2.5 per cent of the 13.5 million homes who took the system paying and watching the performance.

MICHAEL JACKSON

♦ It is now common knowledge that Michael Jackson's *Thriller* album, which topped the US chart for 37 weeks, is the biggest-selling record of all time with world sales of over 40 million. However, few people realise that not only was it Michael's first no. 1 album ever in the US or UK (including his days

with the **Jackson Five**) but it was also the first LP by a black act to top the pop charts on either side of the Atlantic for three years. Incidentally, *Thriller* also helped to make Michael Jackson the first artist ever to simultaneously top the US pop singles and album charts, black singles and albums charts and the dance chart.

♦ *The Making of Michael Jackson's 'Thriller'* was the first music video to go gold and also the first to go platinum.

♦ Both **Barbra Streisand** and **Whitney Houston** reportedly turned down the chance of singing with him on the track 'I Just Can't Stop Loving You'. The record of course went on to be a transatlantic no. 1 when recorded with session singer and writer

Siedah Garrett. Siedah, who has sung backing vocals on four **Madonna** no. 1s, was later a host on TV's *America's Top 10*.

♦ Another record Michael Jackson holds is that he was the first act to have an album enter both the UK and US charts at the no. 1 position – a feat achieved by *Bad* in 1987. Incidentally, it sold over 2 million copies in its first week Stateside, while in its first week in Britain it sold over 340 000 LPs and 40 000 CDs, which is not only the record sale for a week but was also more than four times the sales of the week's no. 1 single ('Never Gonna Give You Up' by Rick Astley).

♦ Michael was the first entertainer to earn over $100 million in one year and was presented with a unique award by his label CBS for selling over 110 million records in the 1980s, making him the biggest-selling artist of the decade.

MADONNA

♦ **Madonna** was the first woman to hold down the top two places on the UK chart with her singles 'Into The Groove' and 'Holiday' in August, 1985.

♦ She set the record for UK Top 10 hits in one year in 1985 with eight, namely 'Like A Virgin', 'Material Girl', 'Crazy For You', 'Into The Groove', 'Holiday', 'Angel', 'Gambler' and 'Dress You Up'.

Since 1984, **Madonna** *has been causing a commotion with her phenomenal success.*

♦ Together with **Whitney Houston** she holds the record for the most no. 1 singles in the US by a female artist with nine.

♦ She is also the only female singer to have had two albums that both contained five different UK Top 40 singles. The LPs were *True Blue* and *Like A Virgin*.

♦ She is the first female singer to have as many as 16 consecutive US Top 5 singles – a run that halted in 1989 when 'Oh Father' only reached no. 19.

♦ She was the most successful singles artist in both the US and UK in the 80s. In the US she had 17 Top 10 hits of which only one failed to make the Top 5. In the UK she notched up 22 Top 10s (only two of which missed the Top 5), had more weeks in the Top 10, and sold more singles than any other act. In 1990 she added a further three Top 10s in both countries.

♦ In the six years prior to the release of her *The Immaculate Collection* album her world sales figures were said to be 54 million albums and 26 million singles – a total which included over six million singles in the UK alone. Only **Elvis** and the **Beatles** sold more records in a similar period of time.

NEW KIDS ON THE BLOCK

♦ In 1990 in the UK **New Kids On The Block** became the first all American group since the **Osmonds**, in 1973, to score three consecutive Top 5 hits.

♦ They were the first US group ever to score six US Top 10 hits in a year – a feat they achieved in 1989. A year later they broke the record in the UK for groups with eight Top 10s – a feat that even the **Beatles** and **Rolling Stones** had not achieved.

♦ The group broke the world record for sponsorship fees when they received over $10 million from McDonald's hamburger chain for sponsorship of their 1990 US tour. They are said to have also picked up a cool $5.5 million for doing two promotions for Pepsi Cola in 1990.

♦ They are also the first act to have sold over a million copies of a music video – they did this with *Hangin' Tough Live* in 1990. In the same year the group's previous video *Hangin' Tough* and their *Step By Step* also passed the magic million mark.

♦ A dubious record that the group holds is having the smallest selling UK no. 1 for 20 years with 'Hangin' Tough', which held the top spot in 1990 after selling only 30 000 copies in a week – less than half that an average chart topper usually sells.

♦ They earn much extra money from the merchandising of items like New Kids hats, towels, lunch boxes, party supplies, stationery, sleeping bags, dolls, puzzles and hair care products.

♦ If you thought you recognised some of NKOTB's dance steps, it could be due to the fact that their choreographer is **Charlie Atkins** who choreographed many of the Motown acts in the 60s.

♦ In 1991 they were involved in a law suit concerning the illegal use of their name, which they hope will bring them over $80 million in damages.

♦ They were the top recording act in both the UK and US in 1990 and their gross earnings between spring, 1989 and the end of 1990 were an amazing $861.37 million (£465 million)!

A Big Mac and a Pepsi are the right stuff for those record-shattering **New Kids On The Block**.

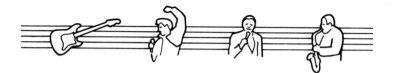

PLAY THAT FUNKY MUSIC

BLACK BEATS

♦ The **first blues recording** is said to be **Mamie Smith**'s recording of 'Crazy Blues' which she cut on Valentine's Day in 1920.

♦ The **first authentic reggae artist to hit the US Top 10** was **Desmond Dekker** who made it with 'Israelites' in 1969, and the **first to top the US charts** was **Maxi Priest** in 1990 with 'Close To You'. Texan **Johnny Nash**, a man of many styles, who had worked with **Bob Marley**, had previously topped that chart in 1972 with the pop/reggae hit 'I Can See Clearly Now'.

♦ The influence of reggae music reached its peak in the UK at the end of 1982 when three successive no. 1s were reggae influenced. They were: **Musical Youth**'s 'Pass The Dutchie', **Culture Club**'s 'Do You Really Want To Hurt Me' and **Eddy Grant**'s 'I Don't Wanna Dance'.

♦ In 1986 **Freddie Jackson** became the **first artist to replace himself** at the top of the US black music chart for 29 years when his solo hit, 'Tasty Love', replaced his duet with **Melba Moore**, 'A Little Bit More'. The previous act to achieve this feat had been **Fats Domino** with 'Blueberry Hill' and 'Blue

Monday', in 1957. The **best performance on the black music chart** (or the **Harlem Hit Parade** as it was called then) was in 1946 when **Louis Jordan** held the top four positions on the chart with 'Choo Choo Ch'Boogie', 'Ain't That Just Like A Woman', 'Stone Cold Dead In The Market' and 'That Chicks Too Young To Fry'. Incidentally, the last song was written by **Tommy Edwards**, the **first artist to revive one of his own old hits and see it go even higher** the second time round. The song was 'It's All In The Game' which Tommy took to no. 18 in 1951 and to no. 1 on both sides of the Atlantic in 1958.

♦ The **first no. 1 rap record** in the world was the **Sugarhill Gang**'s 'Rapper's Delight' which topped the pop charts in Canada and Holland in 1980, but surprisingly only reached no. 36 in the US, despite selling over a million copies there. At that time most people in the record business and most record buyers thought this would be the sole rap hit and did not foresee its influence on pop and black music.

♦ On 27th May, 1989, a record four of the top five and six of the top ten black music LPs in the US were by rap acts – namely **De La Soul**, **Slick Rick**, **Tone Loc** and **M.C. Hammer**.

♦ The **US rap singles chart** was introduced on 11th March, 1989, and the first chart topper was 'Self Destruction' by a collection of rap superstars under the name **Stop The Violence Movement**. On 3rd June, 1989, it was decided that only records that contained 100 per cent rap would be included in this chart which had previously included records that featured rap as well as singing.

♦ Probably the **most new entries on a national chart** occurred when the **dance charts** used in *Music Week* changed its compilation source in December, 1990. This change of compilers resulted in 38 of the Top 60 singles entering the chart for the first time, not to mention six of the Top 10 albums. The following week the top three singles were all new entries as were another three of the Top 10.

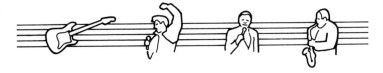

ALIVE AND KICKING

CONCERTS/APPEARANCES

♦ **Gene Vincent**'s first European visit was not in late 1959 as many think, but in January, 1954, when he was a sailor in the US navy. In the same year another late 50s US rock star visited Britain for the first time – **Ricky Nelson**, who 'took in' the sights and 'took out' the girls during his vacation.

♦ **Jimi Hendrix**, who set his first guitar alight on 31st March, 1967, launched his group the **Band Of Gypsys** at the Filmore East venue in New York on New Year's Eve, 1969.

♦ The first **Glastonbury Festival** was held in 1971 and the first **Donnington Festival** was held a decade later.

♦ The first of country star **Willie Nelson**'s famous 4th July Picnic shows was staged in 1973.

♦ One time child star **Lena Zavaroni** holds the dubious honour of being the only artist to appear twice on BBC TV's top-rated *Top Of The Pops* when she was not in the UK chart. She was also the last artist that the ultra successful Memphis-based soul label **Stax** heavily promoted before they folded in 1974. Despite the huge promotion campaign for the nine-year-old's single 'Ma, He's Making Eyes At Me' it got no higher than no. 91 Stateside.

♦ The longest running musical ever on Broadway was the 50s orientated *Grease* which ran for 3883 performances and grossed $8 million before closing on 13th

April, 1980. In Japan the British show *Cats* holds the record with 1590 performances there playing to 92 per cent capacity houses and seen by 1.6 million people.

♦ US rock group **Kiss**' first show *without* make-up was on 18th September, 1983, when they made an appearance on MTV.

♦ Probably the only artist to make his live debut with his 'Farewell Show' was **neil** (actor-singer **Nigel Planer**). Neil, who had a no. 2 UK hit with 'Hole In My Shoe' (originally recorded by 60s group **Traffic**) played his only show at the prestigious Hammersmith Odeon in 1984.

♦ **Bananarama**, who first hit the UK chart in February, 1982, and have charted regularly since then, waited until May, 1989, for their first tour. It was a success but oddly, they have not fared so well on the charts since. The **Pet Shop Boys** also waited a long time before performing live. Their first hit came in late 1985 and they finally hit the road four years later. **Kate Bush** on the other hand, successfully toured in 1979, but despite much success around the world she has not hit the road since.

♦ The first major heavy metal festival in Moscow took place in August, 1989, and starred Americans **Bon Jovi** and **Motley Crue** and Britain's **Ozzy**

Osbourne. It was a big success and was also seen by many millions on US 'pay' TV. Shortly after this, the **Who**'s comeback US tour was similarly shown on US pay TV and surprisingly attracted only 1.2 per cent of the possible audience.

♦ **Ringo Starr**'s first US Tour since the **Beatles** happened in August, 1989. Included amongst the musicians on the road with him were **Nils Lofgren, Clarence Clemons, Levon Helm, Rick Danko, Billy Preston, Joe Walsh** and **Dr. John**.

♦ It took 30 years for Lubbock, Texas to honour their best known 'son' **Buddy Holly** with a music festival. It took place in October, 1989, and was sponsored by the soft drinks giant **Dr. Pepper** whose name took precedence over Buddy's in the billing. Also in Texas that month **Roy Orbison**, who had died less than a year before, had his name added to the West Texas Walk Of Fame (a walkway where many stars have their names put on paving slabs).

♦ The record for appearances at the prestigious **Madison Square Gardens** in New York is held by **Elton John**, who performed there for the 30th time in October, 1989.

MONEY GO ROUND

MUSICAL NOTES

♦ In 1955 **RCA Victor** paid **Sun Records** $40 000 for **Elvis**, of which only $5000 was paid to Elvis.

♦ The **Original Cast** album of *My Fair Lady* sold 5 million copies worldwide in 1957, which was more than any previous LP. **CBS Inc.**, who had financed the show for $500 000, earned $32 million from it.

♦ The size of record deals has always fascinated and amazed the record-buying public. Back in 1959, Britons were astounded to hear that skiffle singer **Lonnie Donegan** was to get an advance of £10 000 ($25 000) from **Pye Records**. Four years later, **Ricky Nelson** received $1 million (£435 000) from **Decca**. Of course, these figures fade into insignificance when compared to the cool $13 million **Stevie Wonder** picked up in 1976 for re-signing to **Motown**. A decade later, the **Rolling Stones** received $25 million to join **Columbia** (CBS). Like film box office records these 'transfer fee' records are constantly being broken. However, all the figures you read should be taken with a large cup full of salt since record companies and artists like to impress the public by exaggerating the amount of money that has changed hands.

♦ Advancing advances: In the late 1960s, the top rate for an artist in the US was about $150 000 per album. Then, in 1970, **Neil Diamond** did well for himself by getting $425 000 per album for a ten album deal with **CBS**. Six years later, they paid **James Taylor** $1 million per album as well as a $2.5 million advance. In 1987 their contracts for **Billy Joel** and **Bruce**

David Bowie *picked up a fair day's pay for a fair day's work!*

Springsteen were for $2 million per album.

♦ **Jean-Michel Jarre** released only one copy of his album *Music For Supermarkets* which he sold at auction for £5800 ($9000).

♦ **Buddy Holly**'s glasses, which were discovered in 1980 (21 years after his fatal air crash) at the police station at Mason City, Iowa were sold for $45 000 (£28 000) in 1990.

♦ In 1983 both **David Bowie** and **Van Halen** picked up $1.5 million dollars (£950 000) for one performance at the US Festival.

♦ **John Lennon**'s widow **Yoko Ono** gave £250 000 ($400 000) to a Liverpool old folks home in January, 1984. It was of course Strawberry Fields, which had been immortalised in the **Beatles**' song 'Strawberry Fields Forever'. Incidentally, later that year an old school exercise book of **John**'s sold at auction for £18 000 ($28 000).

♦ The famous **Motown Records** studio **Hitsville**, in Detroit (where all of their 60s hits were recorded) was sold for $50 million in July, 1989, to the New York-based company **Soundworks**.

THE NEXT TIME

ONE HIT WONDERS

♦ Acts whose only chart entry was a number one record are not uncommon and we felt it was time for a list of their follow up's – those 'important' records that no doubt both they and their record companies felt sure would also zoom up to the top spot too . . .

ARTIST	NO. 1 HIT	FOLLOW UP 'FLOP'
KITTY KALLEN	LITTLE THINGS MEAN A LOT (UK, 1954)	THE SPIRIT OF CHRISTMAS
DREAMWEAVERS	IT'S ALMOST TOMORROW (UK, 1956)	A LITTLE LOVE CAN GO A LONG, LONG WAY
KALIN TWINS	WHEN (UK, 1958)	FORGET ME NOT
SILHOUETTES	GET A JOB (US, 1958)	HEADIN' FOR THE POOR HOUSE
ELEGANTS	LITTLE STAR (US, 1958)	PLEASE BELIEVE ME
JERRY KELLER	HERE COMES SUMMER (UK, 1959)	IF I HAD A GIRL
RICKY VALANCE	TELL LAURA I LOVE HER (UK 1960)	MOVIN' AWAY

ARTIST	NO. 1 HIT	FOLLOW UP 'FLOP'
HOLLYWOOD ARGYLES	ALLEZ-OOP (US 1960)	GUN TOTTIN' CRITTER CALLED JACK
B. BUMBLE	NUT ROCKER (UK 1962)	APPLE KNOCKER
SINGING NUN	DOMINIQUE (US 1963)	TOUS LES CHEMINS
OVERLANDERS	MICHELLE (UK 1966)	MY LIFE
ZAGER & EVANS	IN THE YEAR 2525 (UK 1969)	MISTER TURN KEY
ARCHIES	SUGAR SUGAR (UK 1969)	JINGLE JANGLE
NORMAN GREENBAUM	SPIRIT IN THE SKY (UK 1970)	CANNED HAM
CLIVE DUNN	GRANDAD (UK 1971)	MY LADY (NANA)
FLOATERS	FLOAT ON (UK 1977)	YOU DON'T HAVE TO SAY YOU LOVE ME
BRIAN & MICHAEL	MATCHSTALK MEN & MATCHSTALK CATS & DOGS (UK 1978)	EVENSONG
ANITA WARD	RING MY BELL (UK 1979)	DON'T DROP MY LOVE
LENA MARTELL	ONE DAY AT A TIME (UK 1979)	SOMEWHERE IN MY LIFETIME
M	POP MUZIK (US 1979)	MOONLIGHT & MUZAK
JOE DOLCE	SHADDUP YOU FACE (UK 1981)	IF YOU WANNA BE HAPPY
CHARLENE	I'VE NEVER BEEN TO ME (UK 1982)	IF I COULD SEE MYSELF
PHYLLIS NELSON	MOVE CLOSER (UK 1985)	I LIKE YOU
ROBIN BECK	THE FIRST TIME (UK 1988)	SAVE UP ALL YOUR TEARS

♦ It has been said that the hardest thing for an artist in the pop business to do is to try and repeat the success of their biggest (and often only) hit. Obviously no performer wants to be known as a 'one-hit wonder' or to see their successful career start to tail off. In the days before albums took over, when the single was 'king', it was therefore not unusual for an act (especially those in the US) to try every trick they knew to repeat their one, or biggest success. This often meant trying to duplicate many of the ingredients that helped them get that hit. Several of the acts listed below did have other hits but the unlucky ones never managed to return to the winners' circle.

* = only big hit

ACT	HIT TITLE	LATER RECORD(S)
LEE ALLEN	WALKIN WITH MR. LEE*	TWISTIN' WITH MR. LEE
PAUL ANKA	DIANA	REMEMBER DIANA
AQUATONES	YOU*	FOR YOU FOR YOU
LAVERN BAKER	JIM DANDY	JIM DANDY GOT MARRIED
KENNY BALL	MIDNIGHT IN MOSCOW	FROM RUSSIA WITH LOVE
BILL BLACK'S COMBO	SMOKIE	SON OF SMOKIE
BOBBETTES	MR. LEE*	I SHOT MR. LEE
GARY U.S. BONDS	NEW ORLEANS	TAKE ME BACK TO NEW ORLEANS
ROY BROWN	MISS FANNY BROWN	MISS FANNY BROWN RETURNS
DORSEY BURNETTE	TALL OAK TREE*	LITTLE ACORN
ROY 'C'	SHOTGUN WEDDING*	THE WEDDING IS OVER
ACE CANNON	TUFF*	RUFF
CAPRIS	THERE'S A MOON OUT TONIGHT*	THERE'S A MOON OUT AGAIN
CASCADES	RHYTHM OF THE RAIN*	MAYBE THE RAIN WILL FALL
CHAMPS	TEQUILA	TOO MUCH TEQUILA
CHARLIE & RAY	I LOVE YOU MADLY*	MAD WITH YOU BABY
JIMMY CLANTON	JUST A DREAM	JUST A MOMENT

ACT	HIT TITLE	LATER RECORD(S)
COZY COLE	TOPSY (PT 2)*	TURVY (PT 2)
ARTHUR CONLEY	SWEET SOUL MUSIC	MORE SWEET SOUL MUSIC
CRAZY ELEPHANT	GIMME GIMME GOOD LOVIN'*	GIMME SOME MORE
CRESTS	16 CANDLES	YOU BLEW OUT THE CANDLES
DELLS	OH WHAT A NIGHT	OH WHAT A GOOD NIGHT
DREAMLOVERS	WHEN WE GET MARRIED*	MAY I KISS THE BRIDE
CLEVE DUNCAN & THE PENGUINS	EARTH ANGEL*	YOU'RE AN ANGEL
DUANE EDDY	REBEL ROUSER	SON OF REBEL ROUSER
EDSELS	RAMA LAMA DING DONG*	SHADDY DADDY DIP DIP
FALCONS	YOU'RE SO FINE*	FINE FINE FINE
LARRY FINEGAN	DEAR ONE*	DEAR ONE (PT 2)
FIREFLIES	YOU WERE MINE (AT THE TIME)*	YOU WERE MINE (FOR A WHILE)
JIMMY GILMER	SUGAR SHACK	SUGAR IN THE WOODS
JAMES GILREATH	LITTLE BAND OF GOLD*	PEARLS GOLD & SILVER
BILL HALEY	ROCK AROUND THE CLOCK	DANCE AROUND THE CLOCK
SLIM HARPO	I'M A KING BEE	LITTLE QUEEN BEE
WILBERT HARRISON	KANSAS CITY*	GOODBYE KANSAS CITY
BILL HAYES	THE BALLAD OF DAVY CROCKETT*	THE LEGEND OF WYATT EARP
BOBBY HEBB	SUNNY*	MY PRETTY SUNSHINE
HUDSON & LANDRY	AJAX LIQUOR STORE*	AJAX MORTUARY
		AJAX PET STORE
ISLEY BROTHERS	TWIST & SHOUT	SURF & SHOUT
JAN & DEAN	BABY TALK	SHE'S STILL TALKING BABY TALK
JAN & DEAN	SURF CITY	FOLK CITY
JOHNNIE & JOE	OVER THE MOUNTAIN (ACROSS THE SEA)*	ACROSS THE SEA
JOE JONES	YOU TALK TOO MUCH*	ONE BIG MOUTH
JERRY KELLER	HERE COMES SUMMER*	SOME SUMMER
MOE KOFFMAN	SWINGIN' SHEPHERD BLUES*	SWINGIN' SHEPHERD BLUES TWIST
JACKIE LEE	THE DUCK*	THE SHOTGUN AND THE DUCK THE CHICKEN
BOBBY LEWIS	TOSSIN' AND TURNIN'	I'M TOSSIN' AND TURNIN' AGAIN
LITTLE JOE & THE THRILLERS	PEANUTS*	PEANUTS AND POPCORN
LITTLE WILLIE LITTLEFIELD	K.C. LOVIN'	MISS K.C.'S FINE
LOST GENERATION	THE SLY, THE SLICK AND THE WICKED*	THE YOUNG, THE TOUGH AND THE WICKED
NATHANIEL MAYER & FABULOUS TWILIGHTS	THE VILLAGE OF LOVE*	GOING BACK TO THE VILLAGE OF LOVE
STICKS McGHEE	DRINKING WINE SPO-DEE-O-DEE*	DRANK UP ALL THE WINE LAST NIGHT
BYRON McGREGOR	AMERICANS*	THANK YOU AMERICA
MONOTONES	BOOK OF LOVE*	READING THE BOOK OF LOVE
LOU MONTE	PEPINO THE ITALIAN MOUSE	PEPINO'S FRIEND PASQUEL
SANDY NELSON	LET THERE BE DRUMS	LET THERE BE DRUMS AND BASS
SANDY NELSON	TEEN BEAT	TEEN BEAT '65
CLIFF NOBLES & CO.	THE HORSE*	PONY THE HORSE
		HITCH IT TO THE HORSE
		HORSE FEVER
PAUL & PAULA	HEY PAULA	DEAR PAULA
ED PAULING & 5 ROYALES	BABY DON'T DO IT	NOW BABY DON'T DO IT

ACT	HIT TITLE	LATER RECORD(S)
GARY PAXTON/HOLLY- WOOD ARGYLES	ALLEZ OOP*	ALLEZ OOP WAS A TWO DAB MAN
BOBBY 'BORIS' PICKET	MONSTER MASH*	MONSTER MAN JAM MONSTER CONCERT MONSTER SWIM
PINKERTONS	MIRROR MIRROR*	BEHIND THE MIRROR
PRESTON EPPS	BONGO ROCK*	BONGO ROCKET MISTER BONGOS B-WANA BONGOS
LLOYD PRICE	LADY LUCK	OH LADY LUCK
PAUL REVERE & THE RAIDERS	LIKE LONGHAIR	LIKE BLUEGRASS
MARTY ROBBINS	EL PASO	EL PASO CITY
FLOYD ROBINSON	MAKING LOVE*	THE ART OF MAKING LOVE
ROCKIN' REBELS	WILD WEEKEND*	ANOTHER WILD WEEKEND
ROYAL GUARDSMEN	SNOOPY VS THE RED BARON	SNOOPY VS THE BLACK KNIGHT
ROYAL PHILHARMONIC ORCHESTRA	HOOKED ON CLASSICS*	HOOKED ON AMADEUS (and many other HOOKED ON ...)
RUMBLERS	BOSS*	BOSS SOUL
CHARLIE RYAN	HOT ROD LINCOLN*	HOT ROD HADES HOT ROD GUITAR HOT ROD RACE
SHERRYS	POP POP POPEYE*	MONK MONK MONKEY
STRING-A-LONGS	WHEELS	SPINNIN' MY WHEELS
SURFARIS	WIPE OUT*	PSYCHE-OUT KICK OUT
T. TEXAS TYLER	DECK OF CARDS	THE SOLDIER'S PRAYER BOOK
TONY & JOE	THE FREEZE*	TWIST AND FREEZE
TOYS	A LOVER'S CONCERTO	MY LOVE SONATA
JESSIE LEE TURNER	THE LITTLE SPACE GIRL*	I'M THE LITTLE SPACE GIRL'S FATHER
VELOURS	CAN I COME OVER TONIGHT	CAN I WALK YOU HOME
LARRY VERNE	MR. CUSTER*	I'M A BRAVE LITTLE SOLDIER THE COWARD THAT WON THE WEST RETURN OF MR. CUSTER
BOBBY VINTON	ROSES ARE RED	RED ROSES FOR MOM THE LAST ROSE
MARY WELLS	TWO LOVERS	TWO LOVERS' HISTORY
MERI WILSON	TELEPHONE MAN*	PETER THE METER READER
SHEB WOOLEY	PURPLE PEOPLE EATER*	SANTA AND THE PURPLE PEOPLE EATER
LINK WRAY	RUMBLE	RUMBLE MAMBO
JOHN ZACHERELE	DINNER WITH DRAC(ULA)*	MONSTERS HAVE PROBLEMS TOO (and many other MONSTER titles)

OLD GOLD

♦ When music historians look back on the last ten years of the British charts they will notice that it was a decade when many old records returned to the UK charts in their original form, while others were re-mixed and scored again.

♦ The slowest journey to the no. 1 position in the UK was that of the late **Jackie Wilson**'s 'Reet

Petite' which first entered the chart on 15th November, 1957, and finally made no. 1 on 27th December, 1986, over 29 years later! Incidentally, it was the first hit composed by **Berry Gordy Jr.**, the founder of Motown – and it never even reached the Top 40 in the US.

♦ Most of the many 'oldies' that have charted did so after being used in TV commercials. In 1990 two very old US no. 1 singles hit the Top 3 in the UK after being heard on TV. Firstly there was the **Steve Miller Band**'s 1973 hit 'The Joker', and then came **Bobby Vinton**'s even older 'Blue Velvet' from 1963. An odd connection between the two records is that US R&B/Doo-Wop group the **Clovers** charted in the US before Bobby with 'Blue Velvet' in 1955, and that lines taken straight from one of that group's biggest hits 'Lovey Dovey' appear on Steve's hit.

♦ Other old US hits brought to

Jackie Wilson's *1957 debut hit took over 29 years to top the UK chart.*

the UK chart courtesy of TV commercials include 60s soul singles 'When A Man Loves A Woman' by **Percy Sledge**, 'Stand By Me' by **Ben E. King**, 'Wonderful World' by **Sam Cooke** and 'I Heard It Through The Grapevine' by **Marvin Gaye** – all UK Top 10s in the mid-80s thanks to commercials for Levis 501 jeans. Incidentally, the versions of the latter two songs heard in the ads were not by the acts concerned but by 'sound-a-like' British session singer **Tony Jackson**, a member of **Paul Young**'s backing group and one time member of **Sweet Dreams**, who hit in the UK with 'Honey Honey' in 1974.

♦ The power of TV also made **Nina Simone**'s 1959 recording of 'My Baby Just Cares For Me' a belated Top 5 hit in 1987, after it was heard in a perfume commercial. The longest gap between a record first hitting and then returning to the Top 20 was nearly 31 years set by **Nat 'King' Cole**'s big 1957 hit 'When I Fall In Love', which was re-issued to challenge the new version by **Rick Astley**. A more unusual occurrence happened in 1976 when a 19-year-old flop 'Jungle Rock' brought unknown Florida-based R 'n' R singer **Hank Mizell** to the UK and Dutch Top 10s. Incidentally, none of these tracks had ever charted in the US where they originated.

♦ It's not unusual for an artist's first release to have no chart success initially but when re-issued, after they have actually had a hit with a different record, it shoots up the charts. Examples of this include **Bros**' 'I Owe You Nothing', **Wham!**'s 'Wham Rap' and **Paul Young**'s 'Love Of The Common People'.

♦ For the record, a record nine of the UK Top 40 singles on 21st September, 1985, were re-issued records.

♦ Apart from the records mentioned above the following re-issues charted for a second time in the UK since 1980:

HIT TITLE	ACT	FIRST CHARTED	HIT AGAIN (Top 20)
LOVE ME DO	THE BEATLES	1962	1982
HOUSE OF THE RISING SUN	THE ANIMALS	1964	1982
JAILHOUSE ROCK	ELVIS PRESLEY	1958	1983
LOVE WILL TEAR US APART	JOY DIVISION	1980	1983
THINKING OF YOU	SISTER SLEDGE	1979	1984
LOST IN MUSIC	SISTER SLEDGE	1979	1984
BORDERLINE	MADONNA	1984	1985
LITTLE RED CORVETTE	PRINCE	1983	1985
1999	PRINCE	1983	1985
THEME FROM NEW YORK, NEW YORK	FRANK SINATRA	1980	1986
ROCK LOBSTER	B-52s	1979	1986
I GET THE SWEETEST FEELING	JACKIE WILSON	1968	1987
IT'S NOT UNUSUAL	TOM JONES	1965	1987
HIGHER AND HIGHER	JACKIE WILSON	1967	1987
OOPS UPSIDE YOUR HEAD	GAP BAND	1980	1987
VALERIE	STEVE WINWOOD	1982	1987
I FOUND LOVIN'	FATBACK BAND	1984	1987
HOT IN THE CITY	BILLY IDOL	1982	1988
C'MON EVERYBODY	EDDIE COCHRAN	1959	1988
HE AIN'T HEAVY HE'S MY BROTHER	HOLLIES	1969	1988
EASY	COMMODORES	1977	1988
UNCHAINED MELODY	RIGHTEOUS BROTHERS	1965	1990
YOU'VE LOST THAT LOVIN' FEELING	RIGHTEOUS BROTHERS	1965	1990
(I'VE HAD) THE TIME OF MY LIFE	MEDLEY/WARNES	1987	1991

The following hits went into the Top 20 in Britain in re-mixed forms:

HIT TITLE	ACT	HIT	HIT AGAIN
KNOCK ON WOOD	AMII STEWART	1979	1985
HEAVEN MUST BE MISSING AN ANGEL	TAVARES	1976	1986
YOU TO ME ARE EVERYTHING	REAL THING	1976	1986
CAN'T GET BY WITHOUT YOU	REAL THING	1976	1986
YOU SEXY THING	HOT CHOCOLATE	1975	1987
CARS	GARY NUMAN	1979	1987

HIT TITLE	ACT	HIT	HIT AGAIN
JACK LE FREAK	CHIC	1978	1987
I WANT YOU BACK	JACKSON FIVE	1970	1988
IN THE AIR TONIGHT	PHIL COLLINS	1981	1988
LOVELY DAY	BILL WITHERS	1978	1988
DOWNTOWN	PETULA CLARK	1964	1988
FAKE	ALEXANDER O'NEAL	1987	1988
I'M EVERY WOMAN	CHAKA KHAN	1978	1989
POP MUZIK	M	1979	1989
NEVER TOO MUCH	LUTHER VANDROSS	1983	1989
THE TIME WARP	DAMIAN	1987	1989
AIN'T NOBODY	RUFUS & CHAKA KHAN	1984	1989
I'M STILL WAITING	DIANA ROSS	1976	1990
BLACK BETTY	RAM JAM	1977	1990
ENGLISHMAN IN NEW YORK	STING	1988	1990

♦ Apart from these, 'megamixes' of their previous hits made the Top 20 for **Alexander O'Neal**, **Bobby Brown**, **Olivia Newton-John & John Travolta**, and **Technotronic**. Amazingly, none of these re-mixed singles even made the US Top 100!

♦ It's unusual for old records to make the US charts, a fact which made 13th May, 1989, an exceptional day because there were four old singles in the Top 100. The records were 'Iko Iko' by the **Belle Stars** (which had been a UK hit in 1982), 'Where Are You Now' from **Jimmy Harnen & Synch** (which previously charted in the US in 1986), 'Into The Night' by **Benny Mardones** (a Top 20 hit in both 1980 and '89) and a re-recording of 'Send Me An Angel' by Australian group **Real Life** (a Top 40 hit in 1983).

♦ Soulful white singer **Timi Yuro**, who had a big US hit with 'Hurt' in 1961, had to wait two decades until that single became a hit in Europe – it made the Top 10 in Holland in 1981.

♦ In August, 1986, two old hits from 1964 returned to the charts. In Britain it was **Lulu**'s recording of 'Shout' and in the US it was the **Beatles'** version of 'Twist & Shout'. Co-incidentally, both of these 'shout' songs had originally been hits for the **Isley Brothers**.

♦ One of the oddest coincidences in UK pop music is that two songs that stood together in the Top 10 in 1959 both returned together to the Top 10 in 1986, and both of the new hits featured the original performers. The records concerned were 'Living Doll' (recorded by **Cliff Richard** in 1959 and by him and the **Young Ones** in 1986) and 'Peter Gunn' (a **Duane Eddy** hit in 1959 and by him with **Art Of Noise** in 1986!).

♦ Oddly, the UK's 1950s rock 'n' roll revival acts **Darts** and **Showaddywaddy** in the 1970s and **Shakin' Stevens** in the 80s all had more UK hits than the following rock 'n' roll greats: **Chuck Berry**, **Jerry Lee Lewis**, **Eddie Cochran**, **Fats Domino** and **Carl Perkins**.

BITS AND PIECES

ONLY 16

♦ The following is a list of classic records that peaked at no. 16 on the UK or US charts:

TITLE (YEAR OF HIT)	ARTIST	COMMENT
AIN'T THAT A SHAME (1955)	FATS DOMINO	US peak position of his first pop hit
BE BOP-A-LULA and BLUE JEAN BOP (1956)	GENE VINCENT	His two biggest UK hits in the 50s
SWEET LITTLE 16 (1958)	CHUCK BERRY	His biggest UK hit in the 50s
VENUS (1959)	FRANKIE AVALON	US teen idol's biggest UK hit
SWEETS FOR MY SWEET (1961)	DRIFTERS	US peak of the original hit version of the Searcher's smash
PIPELINE (1963)	CHANTAYS	UK's first 'surf music' hit
MISS YOU (1963)	JIMMY YOUNG	Last of seven UK Top 20 hits for the singer turned radio DJ
MAKE IT EASY ON YOURSELF (1965)	WALKER BROTHERS	US peak of UK no. 1 by US act
LADY GODIVA (1966)	PETER & GORDON	Last of their six UK Top 20 hits
ITCHYCOO PARK (1967)	SMALL FACES	Peak position of their only US hit
RAG MAMA RAG (1970)	BAND	Their biggest hit in both UK and US
GET DOWN & GET WITH IT (1971)	SLADE	Their first UK hit
WALK ON THE WILD SIDE (1973)	LOU REED	US peak of the rock classic
IT'S ONLY ROCK 'N' ROLL (1974)	ROLLING STONES	US peak of the rock classic
FIRST IMPRESSIONS (1975)	IMPRESSIONS	Only UK hit for top US group
RIDE A WILD HORSE (1975)	DEE CLARK	His sole UK Top 20 which came 16 years after his sole US hit

TITLE (YEAR OF HIT)	ARTIST	COMMENT
IT'S A GAME (1977)	BAY CITY ROLLERS	Last of their 11 UK Top 20 hits
THE GAMBLER (1978)	KENNY ROGERS	US peak of the song that led to three films for Kenny
THE PRINCE (1979)	MADNESS	The first of 21 Top 20 hits
ORCHARD ROAD (1983)	LEO SAYER	Last of 11 UK Top 20 hits
HOLIDAY (1983)	MADONNA	US peak of her first hit
SEVEN SEAS (1984)	ECHO & THE BUNNYMEN	Last of their five UK Top 20 hits
BROTHERS IN ARMS (1985)	DIRE STRAITS	Title track of UK's all time top-selling LP
THAT'S WHAT FRIENDS ARE FOR (1985)	DIONNE & FRIENDS	UK peak of US no. 1 smash
NO ONE IS TO BLAME (1986)	HOWARD JONES	The last of his nine UK Top 20 hits

Chuck Berry, *the rock 'n' roll legend who only had one sweet little UK Top 20 hit in the rockin' 50s.*

ALL CREATURES GREAT AND SMALL

♦ Believe it or not, there have been scores of solo artists who have not used their surnames on their records but simply prefixed their christian names with the adjectives **Little** or **Big**.
Try these for size:

LITTLE ALFRED
LITTLE ALICE
LITTLE ARCHIE
LITTLE AXE
LITTLE BARBARA
LITTLE BERNIE
LITTLE BETTY
LITTLE BO BITCH
LITTLE BOB
LITTLE BOBBY
LITTLE BONES
LITTLE BOOKER
LITTLE BUCK
LITTLE BUSTER
LITTLE BUTCHIE
LITTLE BUTTER
LITTLE CHARLIE
LITTLE CHERYL
LITTLE CINDY
LITTLE CLARKIE
LITTLE DANNY
LITTLE DAVID
LITTLE DION
LITTLE EDDIE
LITTLE EDITH
LITTLE ESTHER
LITTLE EVA
LITTLE FLOYD
LITTLE GIGI
LITTLE GINNY
LITTLE HANK
LITTLE HELEN
LITTLE HERMAN
LITTLE HOOKS
LITTLE JANICE
LITTLE JEWEL

LITTLE JO
LITTLE JO ANN
LITTLE JOHN
LITTLE JULIAN
LITTLE JULIUS
LITTLE KIRK
LITTLE LARRY
LITTLE LEE
LITTLE LENNY
LITTLE LEROY
LITTLE LINDA
LITTLE LISA
LITTLE MACK
LITTLE MAXINE
LITTLE MILLET
LITTLE MILTON
LITTLE MOJO
LITTLE MUMMY
LITTLE NAT
LITTLE NATALIE
LITTLE OTIS
LITTLE RAY
LITTLE RICHARD
LITTLE RICHIE
LITTLE ROBBY
LITTLE RONNIE
LITTLE ROSE
LITTLE SISTER
LITTLE SONNY
LITTLE STEVE
LITTLE STEVEN
LITTLE SYLVIA
LITTLE T
LITTLE TOM
LITTLE TOMMY
LITTLE TONY

LITTLE TWITCH
LITTLE VICTOR
LITTLE WALLY
LITTLE WALTER
LITTLE WINSTON
LITTLE WOO WOO

BIG AMOS
BIG 'A' RAN
BIG BEN
BIG BLACK
BIG BOB
BIG BOPPER
BIG BUDDY K
BIG DADDY
BIG DAVE
BIG ED
BIG HUGH BABY
BIG IVAN
BIG JACK
BIG JIM

BIG JJ
BIG JOE
BIG KEN
BIG LADY K
BIG LOSER
BIG LOUIS
BIG MAC
BIG MACK
BIG MAYBELLE
BIG PETE
BIG RIC
BIG RIVERS
BIG ROCKER
BIG SAMBO
BIG STEVE
BIG TOM
BIG TONY
BIG WALTER
BIG WILLIE
BIG WOOLFE
BIG YOUTH

Little Eva – *a 'little' artist who made it big.*

*All the **Big Bopper** needed to complete this outfit was a little chantilly lace.*

FOOTBALL CRAZY

♦ Britain is unique in that it it is the only country where sports teams have made the Top 20 singles charts. The list to date (all soccer teams) to achieve this feat is:

TEAM	TITLE	CHART POS	YEAR
ARSENAL FC FIRST TEAM SQUAD	'GOOD OLD ARSENAL'	16	1971
ENGLAND WORLD CUP SQUAD	'BACK HOME'	1	1970
ENGLAND WORLD CUP SQUAD	'THIS TIME'	2	1982
ENGLAND NEW ORDER (with NEW ORDER)	'WORLD IN MOTION'	1	1990
EVERTON 1985	'HERE WE GO'	14	1985
LEEDS UNITED FC	'LEEDS UNITED'	10	1972
LIVERPOOL FC	'WE CAN DO IT'	15	1977
LIVERPOOL FC	'ANFIELD RAP'	3	1988
MANCHESTER UNITED FOOTBALL CLUB	'GLORY GLORY MAN. UNITED'	13	1983
MANCHESTER UNITED FOOTBALL CLUB	'WE ALL FOLLOW MAN. UNITED'	10	1985
SCOTLAND WORLD CUP SQUAD	'EASY EASY'	20	1974
ROD STEWART & SCOTLAND WORLD CUP SQUAD	'OLE OLA'	4	1978
SCOTLAND WORLD CUP SQUAD	'WE HAVE A DREAM'	5	1982
TOTTENHAM HOTSPUR F.A. CUP FINAL SQUAD	'OSSIE'S DREAM'	5	1981
TOTTENHAM HOTSPUR F.A. CUP FINAL SQUAD	'TOTTENHAM TOTTENHAM'	19	1982
(above two featuring Chas & Dave)			
TOTTENHAM HOTSPUR F.A. CUP FINAL SQUAD	'HOT SHOT TOTTENHAM'	18	1987

♦ Only one solo footballer has hit the Top 20 – **Paul Gasgoine**, the star of England's World Cup team in 1990. His record with **Lindisfarne** 'Fog On The Tyne' reached no. 2 in late 1990. The only footballing duo to hit the UK Top 20 were **Glenn** (Hoddle) **and Chris** (Waddle) with 'Diamond Lights' in 1987. Incidentally, Paul, Glenn and Chris all played for London team Tottenham Hotspur who as a team had three Top 20 hits.

IF NOT FOR YOU

♦ Have you ever wondered what would have happened in the pop world without the **Beatles** or the **Rolling Stones**? One thing is for sure – if neither had existed the following records which halted at no. 2 would have gone all the way, thus ensuring that both the songs and the acts would have been forever remembered.

IN THE UK

ARTIST/TITLE	WHO STOPPED THEM
THEM – 'HERE COMES THE NIGHT'	BEATLES
VIKKI CARR – 'IT MUST BE HIM'	BEATLES
EDWIN HAWKINS – 'OH HAPPY DAY'	BEATLES
MIXTURES – 'THE PUSHBIKE SONG'	GEORGE HARRISON
BRIGHOUSE & RASTRICK BAND – 'THE FLORAL DANCE'	PAUL McCARTNEY
BARDO – 'ONE STEP FURTHER'	PAUL McCARTNEY
ENGLAND WORLD CUP SQUAD – 'THIS TIME (WE'LL GET IT RIGHT)'	PAUL McCARTNEY
HOWARD JONES – 'WHAT IS LOVE'	PAUL MCcCARTNEY

IN THE US

ARTHUR BROWN – 'FIRE'	BEATLES
O.C. SMITH – 'LITTLE GREEN APPLES'	BEATLES
COWSILLS – 'HAIR'	BEATLES
MERCY – 'LOVE (CAN MAKE YOU HAPPY)'	BEATLES
JOHNNY CASH – 'A BOY NAMED SUE'	ROLLING STONES
OCEAN – 'PUT YOUR HAND IN THE HAND'	ROLLING STONES
CLINT HOLMES – 'PLAYGROUND IN YOUR MIND'	PAUL McCARTNEY
RICK SPRINGFIELD – 'DON'T TALK TO STRANGERS'	PAUL McCARTNEY

WAR

♦ In answer to the question posed in **Edwin Starr**'s 1970 hit 'War' ('what is it good for?') one answer is 'songs about war'!

Amongst the best-selling records in the US during **World War I** were:

TITLE	ARTIST
IT'S A LONG WAY TO TIPPERARY	JOHN McCORMACK
KEEP THE HOME FIRES BURNING (TILL THE BOYS COME HOME)	FREDERICK J. WHEELER
I DIDN'T RAISE MY BOY TO BE A SOLDIER	MORTON HARVEY
THE STAR SPANGLED BANNER	PRINCE'S ORCHESTRA
PACK UP YOUR TROUBLES IN YOUR OLD KIT BAG	KNICKERBOCKER QUARTET
GOOD-BYE BROADWAY, HELLO FRANCE	AMERICAN QUARTET
OVER THERE	PEERLESS QUARTET
THE BATTLE HYMN OF THE REPUBLIC	CHARLES HARRISON
JUST A BABY'S PRAYER AT TWILIGHT (FOR HER DADDY OVER THERE)	HENRY BURR
HELLO CENTRAL GIVE ME NO MAN'S LAND	AL JOLSON

And during World War II:

TITLE	ARTIST
(LIGHTS OUT) 'TIL REVEILLE	BING CROSBY
THE WHITE CLIFFS OF DOVER	GLENN MILLER
HE WEARS A PAIR OF SILVER WINGS	DINAH SHORE
PRAISE THE LORD AND PASS THE AMMUNITION	MERRY MACS
WHEN THE LIGHTS GO ON AGAIN (ALL OVER THE WORLD)	VAUGHN MONROE
COMIN' IN ON A WING AND A PRAYER	SONG SPINNERS
G.I. JIVE	LOUIS JORDAN
A HOT TIME IN THE TOWN OF BERLIN	ANDREWS SISTERS

ROLL WITH IT

♦ Many rock music books hold US DJ **Alan Freed** responsible for 'inventing' rock 'n' roll music in 1952, others say that he simply coined the phrase that is still in use today. Alan was undoubtedly the first DJ to bring the music to the large US white record-buying public and in doing so he hurried along the worldwide explosion of rock 'n' roll music, but there is no doubt that R&B singers had been rockin' and rollin' before 1952 and that it was only a matter of time before it broke through to the world's record buying public. Here are some examples of US R&B records released *before* Alan started his much lauded radio shows:

TITLE	ARTIST	RELEASE YEAR
DETROIT ROCK	MONTANA TAYLOR	1943
GOOD ROCKIN' TONIGHT	ROY BROWN	1947
ROCKIN' IN RHYTHM	LIONEL HAMPTON	1948
WE'RE GONNA ROCK	WILD BILL MOORE	1948

TITLE	ARTIST	RELEASE YEAR
ROCKIN' BOOGIE	JOE LUTCHER	1948
SHOUT 'N' ROCK	BILLY WILLIAMS	1949
ROCKIN' JENNY JONES	HATTIE NOEL	1949
ROCKIN' AT MIDNIGHT	ROY BROWN	1949
ROCK AND ROLL	WILD BILL MOORE	1949
ROCK THE JOINT	JIMMY PRESTON	1949
ALL SHE WANTS TO DO IS ROCK	WYNONIE HARRIS	1949
ROCKING BLUES	RUTH BROWN	1949
ROCK THE HOUSE	TINY GRIMES	1949
ROCKIN' THE HOUSE	MEMPHIS SLIM	1950
I'M GONNA ROCK	CONNIE JORDAN	1950
WE'RE GONNA ROCK (WE'RE GONNA ROLL)	CECIL GANT	1950
ROCK ME BABY	GREAT GATES	1950
ROCKIN' RHYTHM	PEE WEE BARNUM	1950
ROCKIN' THE BLUES	PEE WEE CRAYTON	1950
ROCK WITH IT	JOHNNY MOORE	1950
SAUSAGE ROCK	DOC SAUSAGE	1950
ROCKIN' WITH RED	PIANO RED	1950
THIS BANDS A ROCKIN'	JOHNNY LEE WILLS	1951
ROLLIN' 'N' ROCKIN'	TOMMY SCOTT	1951
ROCK LITTLE BABY	CECIL GANT	1951
GOOD ROCKIN' MAN	ROY BROWN	1951
ROCKIN' AND ROLLIN'	TOMMY SCOTT	1951
ROCK THE BOOGIE	CECIL GANT	1951
ROCKIN' BOOGIE	LLOYD GLEN	1951
HOW ABOUT ROCKIN' WITH ME	PINEY BROWN	1951
ROCKIN'	ROBINS	1951
LET'S ROCK AWHILE	AMOS MILBURN	1951
ROCKIN' AFTER HOURS	CHUCK NORRIS	1951

♦ According to **Clifford** and **Claude Trenier**, in the summer of 1949, their stage show was often watched closely by the then country singer **Bill Haley**, who after a while asked them what they called the kind of music they were playing – they told him to see the posters which described their group as the **'Rockin' 'n' Rollin' Treniers'**.

♦ This section would not be complete without a mention of 'Rock And Roll' by the **Boswell Sisters**, which was a US no. 7 in 1934. As you may have guessed, it had nothing at all to do with rock.

DON'T BELIEVE THE HYPE

♦ The first hits from **Kim Wilde** and **Bros** – 'Kids In America' and 'When Will I Be Famous' respectively – were both taken off the UK chart for alleged chart hyping (where through dubious means a record gets an exaggerated chart placing). This blow did not stop the records from later reaching the top end of the chart and it did not harm the artists' careers. Kim, in fact, has now scored more hits than her famous dad, **Marty Wilde**. Incidentally, one of Marty's Top 20s, 'Little Girl', was released at the same time as Kim was born!

◆ Other acts who have had records involved in UK chart hyping probes include **Imagination**, **B.A. Robertson**, the **Pinkees**, the **Nolans**, **Barry Manilow** and **Van Halen**.

◆ Probably the most successful 'vocalists' *not* to sing on their records were **Fabrice Morvan** and **Rob Pilatus**, who together were known as **Milli Vanilli**. Their sole album *Girl You Know It's True*, released in 1988, sold an estimated 12 million copies worldwide, topped the US chart, contained four million-selling singles and won the duo a Grammy as Best New Artists of 1989. However, it was announced in late 1990, by their producer **Frank Farian**, that the German-based pair had not actually sung on any part of the album – it was recorded by session singers. Frank, who also owned the name of the act, decided not to record again under that name. It was later revealed that Fab and Rob had previously fronted another group – **Empire Bizarre** – whose recordings they also never actually sang on!
Frank Farian was also the mastermind behind **Boney M**, the German-based black group, who sold tens of millions of records in the 1970s.

◆ Question: What is the connection between **Linda McCartney**, **James Brown**, **David Crosby**, **Harold Melvin**, **Sly Stone**, **Ike Turner** and **Hugh Cornwall** of **The Stranglers**? Answer: In the 80s they all had brushes with the law over drugs.

◆ The only occasion that an artist got a police escort to and from the *Top Of The Pops* studio was in April, 1989, when British rapper **Merlin**, who was serving six months youth custody, was allowed out to perform 'Who's In The House', his single with the **Beatmasters**. Co-incidentally, he had been convicted for house burglary!

◆ In 1990 **Suzanne Vega**'s single 'Tom's Diner' had a backing track added without her (or her record company's) permission by the group **DNA**, who illegally released it before coming to an arrangement with her label and it then went on to be a transatlantic smash. However, this was not the first time something like this had happened – in 1981 Dutch producer **Jaap Eggermont** heard the then current illegal 12-inch 'Bits & Pieces', which included samples of **Beatles**' tracks. He knew instinctively that it was a hit idea and quickly covered the bootleg version using Beatles sound-a-likes, which was legal. The record 'Stars On 45' by **Starsound** (who were called **Stars On 45** in the US) was one of the year's biggest international hits and it started a craze for medleys. This though, was not the first illegal record to inspire a hit – in 1975 one of the biggest records on Britain's Northern Soul scene was 'Footsee' supposedly by an act called the **Sounds Of Soul**. It was actually the instrumental B-side of a late 60s Canadian 'surf' record by a group called the **Chosen Few** – which the bootleggers had speeded up, adding to it the sound of a steam hammer and various crowd noises. The UK record company copied the bootleggers' version (including the crowd noise

Frankie Goes To Hollywood *didn't relax – they had three no. 1 hits in a row.*

from the 1966 F.A. Cup Final) and had a Top 10 hit. Incidentally, the Canadian group were never traced and to this day probably don't know about their much belated success under the name **Wigan's Chosen Few** (the name was changed slightly to avoid confusion with a reggae group).

♦ Wealthy British entertainer **Ken Dodd** had no need for 'Tears' when he was cleared of charges of tax evasion in the late 80s, unlike the less fortunate **Chris Farlowe** (another artist who had a no. 1 hit in the 60s) who ran 'Out Of Time' and was jailed on similar charges in 1983 over a far smaller amount of money.

♦ Ford Motors sued British comedian **Alexei Sayle** over his recording of ''Ullo John Got A New Motor?' which contained references to a Ford Cortina. Ford won the case and the money earned from the record, which peaked at no. 15 in the UK Top 20, was given to charity.

♦ **Danny Bonaduce**, who played **David Cassidy**'s younger brother

in the popular 70s musical TV series *The Partridge Family* was arrested for buying the drug crack in March 1990. However, Danny, who is now a DJ, did not lose his job.

♦ Successful British group of the 60s, **Badfinger**, who hit with records like 'Come And Get It', 'No Matter What' and 'Day After Day' finally won their case against the **Beatles**' Apple Records over unpaid royalties in October, 1985, after an 11-year legal battle. Sadly, by the time of their victory two members **Peter Hamm** and **Tom Evans** had committed suicide.

FRANKIE

♦ Frankie is undoubtedly one of the most popular Christian names among successful singers . . .

♦ **Frankie Goes To Hollywood** were a record breaking group, who like fellow Liverpudlians **Gerry & The Pacemakers** before them, saw their first three releases ('Relax', 'Two Tribes' and 'The Power Of Love') all top the UK chart but their fourth single missed the top spot by just one place (as had **Gerry**'s).

♦ **Frank Ifield** was the first singer to see his first three UK hits reach no. 1 in the UK. They were 'I Remember You', 'Lovesick Blues' and 'Wayward Wind' – all old songs. He had a further four Top 20s, including another no. 1 with the old song 'Confessin''.

♦ **Frankie Laine** is the big-voiced singer from Chicago who spent a record 18 weeks at the top of the UK chart in 1953 with his version of the much recorded religious song 'I Believe'. After 1955 he saw another 11 of his records make the UK Top 20, including the chart-topping 'A Woman In Love' which was one of his 20 US Top 20s.

♦ **Frankie Lymon**, backed by his group **The Teenagers**, not only became the youngest person to top the UK chart but the act also became the first rock group to hit no. 1. They accomplished this in 1956 (when New Yorker Frankie was just 13) with his own song 'Why Do Fools Fall In Love'.

♦ **Frank Sinatra** shares the record for the most Top 10 LPs in the US with 31. He has also had 21 Top 20 UK singles and 31 in the US, including the following Top 5 hits since 1955 – 'Strangers In The Night', 'My Way', 'Theme from New York New York', 'Learnin' The Blues', 'Love And Marriage', 'The Tender Trap', 'That's Life' and 'All The Way'. Incidentally, the UK no. 1 'Frankie' by **Sister Sledge** was written about him by a Swiss-based housewife, **Joy Denny**.

♦ **Frankie Vaughan**, Britain's most successful male singer of the 50s, chalked up 16 UK Top 20s, all cover versions of US recordings. these included two no. 1s: 'Tower Of Strength', originally recorded by **Gene McDaniels**, and 'Garden Of Eden' which was a US hit for **Joe Valino**.

♦ **Frankie Valli** of the **Four Seasons** has notched up several transatlantic solo smashes, including the US no. 1s 'My Eyes Adored You' and 'Grease'.

♦ One of the top US teen idols of the late 50s was **Frankie Avalon** whose 25 hits included the two chart-toppers 'Why' and 'Venus'.

♦ **Frank Chacksfield**, **Frank D'Rone** and **Frank Weir** complete the list of 'Frankies' who made the UK Top 20, and in the US there were also **Frank Mills**, **Frank Pourcel**, **Frank Stallone**, **Franke & The Knockouts** and **Frankie Ford**.

Thirty-one of **Frank Sinatra**'s *albums have gone all the way into the US Top 10.*

The **Barron Knights** *found that seeking chart success in the States was no laughing matter.*

FUNNY?

♦ It's often said that humour doesn't travel and as a rule the same can be said for humorous records. To emphasise this point here is a list of British hit-makers whose 'hilarious' records hit in their homeland but achieved nothing across the ocean.

ARTIST	TITLE	YEAR OF FIRST/ ONLY UK HIT
RUSS ABBOT	A DAY IN THE LIFE OF VINCE PRINCE	1982
'ARMY GAME' TV CAST	ARMY GAME	1958
BARRON KNIGHTS	CALL UP THE GROUPS	1964
BONZO DOG DOO DAH BAND	I'M THE URBAN SPACEMAN	1968
MAX BOYCE	LIVE AT TREORCHY	1975
WILFRED BRAMBELL & HARRY H. CORBETT	AT THE PALACE	1963
THE BRAT	CHALK DUST	1982
BERNARD BRESSLAW	MAD PASSIONATE LOVE	1958
PAUL BURNETTE & DAVE LEE TRAVIS	CONVOY G.B.	1976
TONY CAPSTICK	THE SHEFFIELD GRINDER	1981
JASPER CARROTT	FUNKY MOPED	1975

ARTIST	TITLE	YEAR OF FIRST/ ONLY UK HIT
THE COMMENTATORS	N-N-NINETEEN NOT OUT	1985
BILLY CONNOLLY	D-I-V-O-R-C-E	1975
PETER COOK & DUDLEY MOORE	GOODBYE-EE	1965
TOMMY COOPER	DON'T JUMP OFF THE ROOF DAD	1961
BERNARD CRIBBINS	HOLE IN THE GROUND	1962
HARRY ENFIELD	LOADSAMONEY	1988
KENNY EVERETT	CAPTAIN KREMMEN	1977
THE FIRM	ARTHUR DALEY ('E'S ALRIGHT)	1982
GOODIES	THE IN BETWEENIES	1974
GOONS	I'M WALKING BACKWARDS FOR CHRISTMAS	1956
TONY HANCOCK	THIS IS HANCOCK	1960
BENNY HILL	GATHER IN THE MUSHROOMS	1961
CHRIS HILL	RENTA SANTA	1975
BILLY HOWARD	KING OF THE COPS	1975
MORRIS MINOR & THE MAJORS	STUTTER RAP	1987
NEIL	HOLE IN MY SHOE	1984
'NOT THE NINE O'CLOCK NEWS' CAST	NOT THE NINE O'CLOCK NEWS	1980
ORVILLE THE DUCK	ORVILLE'S SONG	1982
ROLAND RAT	RAT RAPPING	1983
MIKE REID	THE UGLY DUCKLING	1975
PADDY ROBERTS	STRICTLY FOR GROWN-UPS	1959
ALEXEI SAYLE	'ULLO JOHN GOT A NEW MOTOR?	1984
PETER SELLERS	ANY OLD IRON	1957
STAR TURN ON 45 PINTS	STAR TURN ON 45 (PINTS)	1981
STEVE WRIGHT	I'M ALRIGHT	1982
THE WURZELS	COMBINE HARVESTER	1976
YOUNG ONES	LIVING DOLL	1986

♦ However, some American humorists have found that their brand of comedy works well on both sides of the Atlantic. **Shelley Berman**, **Mel Brooks**, **Stan Freeberg**, **Tom Lehrer**, **Bob Newhart**, **Allan Sherman**, **Bobby 'Boris' Pickett** and **Napoleon XIV** have all had transatlantic 'humour hits'. Others, like their British counterparts, have found that their comedy records failed to tickle the UK's funny bone . . .

ARTIST	TITLE	YEAR OF FIRST/ ONLY US HIT
CHEECH & CHONG	BASKETBALL JONES	1971
ANDREW DICE CLAY	DICE	1989
BILLY CRYSTAL	YOU LOOK MARVELLOUS	1985
FRANK FONTAINE	SINGS LIKE CRAZY	1963
DAVE GARDNER	REJOICE DEAR HEARTS	1960

ARTIST	TITLE	YEAR OF FIRST/ ONLY US HIT
DICKIE GOODMAN (& BUCHANAN & GOODMAN)	THE FLYING SAUCER	1956
HOMER & JETHRO	THE BATTLE OF KOOKAMONGA	1959
JOSE JIMINEZ	THE ASTRONAUT	1960
JACKIE MASON	I'M THE GREATEST COMEDIAN IN THE WORLD ONLY NOBODY KNOWS IT YET	1962
STEVE MARTIN	GRANDMOTHER'S SONG	1977
BOB & DOUG McKENZIE	TAKE OFF	1982
NERVOUS NORVUS	TRANSFUSION	1956
MIKE NICHOLS & ELAINE MAY	AN EVENING WITH . . .	1959
JACK ROSS	CINDERELLA	1964
KERMIT SCHAFER	PARDON MY BLOOPER!	1958
SENATOR BOBBY	WILD ONE	1967
RUSTY WARREN	KNOCKERS UP!	1960
ROBIN WILLIAMS	REALITY . . . WHAT A CONCEPT	1979
FLIP WILSON	COWBOYS & COLORED PEOPLE	1967
WOODY WOODBERRY	LOOKS AT LOVE AND LIFE	1960
JOHN ZACHERLE	DINNER WITH DRAC	1958

TRIBUTES

♦ One measure of an artist's importance is to see how many records they are mentioned on or how many have been made about them. These tribute-type records are usually made after a singer's untimely end, although it's not unheard of for records to be made about the real 'kings' whilst they are still alive. Some of these records become hits – see the first section below, while many more fall by the wayside – see the second list.

NAME OF ACT	HIT	LABEL	DATE
DORA BRYAN	'ALL I WANT FOR CHRISTMAS IS A BEATLE'	FONTANA	1963
FOUR PREPS	'A LETTER TO THE BEATLES'	CAPITOL	1964
SWANS	'THE BOY WITH THE BEATLE HAIR'	CAMEO	1964
CAREFREES	'WE LOVE YOU BEATLES'	LONDON	1964
HEINZ	'JUST LIKE EDDIE' (About Eddie Cochran)	DECCA	1963
WILSON PICKETT	'COLE, COOKE AND REDDING'	ATLANTIC	1970
TOMMY DEE/RUBY WRIGHT	'THREE STARS' (About the Buddy Holly plane crash)	CREST/ PARLOPHONE	1959
MIKE BERRY	'TRIBUTE TO BUDDY HOLLY'	HMV	1961
AUDREY	'DEAR ELVIS'	PLUS	1956
RONNIE McDOWELL	'THE KING IS GONE'	SCORPION	1977
DANNY MIRROR	'I REMEMBER ELVIS PRESLEY'	SONET	1977
WILLIAM BELL	A TRIBUTE TO A KING (About Otis Redding)	STAX	1968
LARRY CUNNINGHAM	TRIBUTE TO JIM REEVES	KING	1964

NAME OF ACT	HIT	LABEL	DATE
DEXYS MIDNIGHT RUNNERS	JACKIE WILSON SAID	MERCURY	1982
COMMODORES	NIGHTSHIFT (About Jackie Wilson & Marvin Gaye)	MOTOWN	1985
RIGHTEOUS BROTHERS	ROCK 'N' ROLL HEAVEN (About various dead singers)	HAVEN	1974
JOHNNY CYMBAL	TEENAGE HEAVEN (About various dead singers)	KAPP	1963
TEX RITTER	HILLBILLY HEAVEN (About various dead country singers)	CAPITOL	1961

NAME OF ACT	HIT	LABEL	DATE
FIVE WINGS	JOHNNY'S STILL SINGING (About Johnny Ace)	KING	1955
JOHNNY OTIS	IN MEMORY OF JOHNNY ACE	PEACOCK	1955
PAUL SIMON	LATE GREAT JOHNNY ACE (About Johnny Ace & John Lennon)	WARNER	1983
EXTERMINATORS	BEATLE STOMP/STOMP 'EM OUT	CHANCELLOR	1963
BOB MOLINE	BEATLE STOMP	CHARGER	1964
LIVERS	BEATLE TIME	CONSTELLATION	1964
BENNY & BEDBUGS	THE BEATLE BEAT	DCP	1964
JAPANESE BEATLES	BEATLES SONG (PTS 1 & 2)	GOLDEN CREST	1965
ED SOLOMON	THE BEATLE FLYING SAUCER	DIAMOND	1964
SONNY CURTIS	A BEATLE I WANT TO BE	DIMENSION	1964
STANDELLS	PEPPERMINT BEATLES	LIBERTY	1964
LARRY FINNEGAN	THE OTHER RINGO	RIC	1964
ERNIE MARESCA	THE BEATLE DANCE	RUST	1964
JEKYLL & HYDE	FRANKENSTEIN MEETS THE BEATLES	DCP	1965
JOHNNY & THE HURRICANES	SAGA OF THE BEATLES	JEFF	1964
ROLF HARRIS	RINGO FOR PRESIDENT	COLUMBIA	1964
BONNIE JO MASON (CHER)	RINGO I LOVE YOU/BEATLE BLUES	ANNETTE	1964
BULLDOGS	JOHN, PAUL, GEORGE & RINGO	MGM	1969
BILLY DAVIS	GOODBYE JESSE (About Jesse Belvin)	PEACOCK	1960
SKIP BATTYN	THE BALLAD OF DICK CLARK	SIGNPOST	1972
BILL HAYES	MESSAGE FROM JAMES DEAN	CADENCE	1956
JO ANN CAMPBELL	DUANE (About Duane Eddy)	ABC	1961
EDWIN STARR	MARVIN (About Marvin Gaye)	STREETWAVE	1984
RAY CAMPI	BALLAD OF DONNA & PEGGY SUE (About Buddy Holly & Ritchie Valens)	D	1959
LOCOMOTIONS	LITTLE EVA	GONE	1963
LEE HAZLEWOOD	DOLLY PARTON'S GUITAR	MCA	1979
BILL BLACK'S COMBO	CASHIN' IN (Tribute to Luther Perkins)	HI	1978
LITTLE 'LAMBIE' PENN	I WANNA SPEND CHRISTMAS WITH ELVIS	ATCO	1956
TOM EDWARDS	THE STORY OF ELVIS PRESLEY	CORAL	1957
GREATS	MARCHING ELVIS	EBB	1958
HUNT SISTERS	ELVIS IS ROCKING AGAIN	FORTUNE	1957
MAD MILO	ELVIS FOR CHRISTMAS	MILLION	1957
GARY LEWIS & THE PLAYBOYS	I SAW ELVIS PRESLEY LAST NIGHT	LIBERTY	1969
LARRY & VICKY	SOUL SALUTE TO ELVIS	FRATERNITY	1980

NAME OF ACT	HIT	LABEL	DATE
RAY STEVENS	I SAW ELVIS IN A UFO	MCA	1989
BOBOLINKS	ELVIS PRESLEY'S SERGEANT	KEY	1958
BILLY BOYLE	MY BABY'S JUST CRAZY 'BOUT ELVIS	DECCA	1962
JANIS MARTIN	MY BOY ELVIS	RCA	1956
HUEY LONG	ELVIS STOLE MY GAL	FIDELITY	1962
MILT OSHINS	ALL ABOUT ELVIS	PELVIS	1956
LEON RUSSELL	ELVIS AND MARILYN	PARADISE	1978
CARL PERKINS	THE E.P. EXPRESS	MERCURY	1977
MARK JOHNSON	ODE TO OTIS REDDING	DIAMOND	1968
A. FRIEND	OTIS IS GONE	HOLLYWOOD	1968
BOBBY HARRIS	WE CAN'T BELIEVE YOU'RE GONE (About Otis Redding)	ATLANTIC	1968
DON LANG	THEY CALL HIM CLIFF	HMV	1960
LEE HAZLEWOOD	NANCY AND ME (About Nancy Sinatra)	CAPITOL	1973
LITTLE BARBARA	HANK'S LITTLE FLOWER GIRL (About Hank Williams)	CORAL	1953
VAN MORRISON	JACKIE WILSON SAID	WARNER	1972
BOB EUBANKS	HEAVEN OF THE STARS (About various stars)	TRACY	1961
BILL DUDLEY	TOP TEN IN HEAVEN (About various dead singers)	NASHVILLE	1961

♦ **Geno Washington**, the US soul singer about whom **Dexy's Midnight Runners** sang on their first UK no. 1 'Geno', never had any chart success in his homeland and never had a UK Top 30 single. His only success was with two UK Top 10 LPs which contained mainly cover versions of songs from other black US acts.

GRANDAD

♦ The oldest British female artist to make the UK Top 20 was **Gracie Fields** (born Gracie Stansfield), who was 59 when her recording of 'Around The World' made no. 8 in 1957.

♦ The oldest act to top the US singles chart was **Louis Armstrong**, with 'Hello Dolly' in 1964.

♦ The oldest person to top the UK LP charts with a newly recorded album was US country singer **Slim Whitman**, who did it at the age of 53 in 1977, with his *Red River Valley* LP. Surprisingly, Slim, who had a string of big UK hits in the 50s, has never had a Top 100 LP in his homeland.

♦ The oldest person to appear on a UK Top 20 single is the late **Sir Laurence Olivier**, who spoke on **Paul Hardcastle**'s 1985 UK hit 'Just For Money' when he was 78 years old.

♦ The oldest female group member to have a transatlantic no. 1 is **Grace Slick**, who was 47 when her group **Starship** hit the top with 'Nothing's Gonna Stop Us Now' in 1987.

♦ Annie Mae Bullock (better known as **Tina Turner**) is the oldest female to top the UK LP chart which she achieved with *Foreign Affair* in 1989, when she was 49.

♦ The oldest person to make the UK LP chart was blues great **John Lee Hooker**, whose *Healer* LP

Louis Armstrong *must have thought it a wonderful world in 1964.*

charted in 1990 when he was 72 – it was his first UK charter since 1967. Incidentally, **Bob Dylan**'s first professional appearance was as opening act for John Lee.

♦ The oldest living duo to chart in the UK are **Patrick McNee & Honor Blackman**, whose 1964 recording of 'Kinky Boots' hit the Top 10 in 1990 when they were 68 and 63 years old respectively. **Stan Laurel & Oliver Hardy** were both dead when their mid-30s recording of 'The Trail Of The Lonesome Pine' hit no. 2 in the UK in 1975. Had they lived, they would have been 85 and 83 respectively.

THE YOUNG ONES

♦ The youngest solo artist to enter the UK charts is three-year-old **Ian Doody**, who, under the name **Microbe**, made the UK Top 40 in 1969 with 'Groovy Baby'.

♦ **Rose Marie**, who played Sally (Dick's fellow comedy scriptwriter) in the *Dick Van Dyke TV Show*, had a US chart record as **Baby Rose Marie** in 1932, when she was just 7 years old.

♦ **Petula Clark**, who had a string of transatlantic hits in the 60s, first sang on BBC radio in 1942, when aged just nine. For her appearances that year the BBC, who were not allowed to pay a child, gave her a new party dress.

♦ **Brenda Lee** notched up an amazing 33 US hits including 22 Top 40 hits whilst she was still a teenager. She scored her first hit 'One Step At A Time' in 1957 at the age of 12.

♦ The first teenage male singer to simultaneously top the US single and album charts was **Little Stevie Wonder** in 1963, with 'Fingertips Pt. 2' and *The 12 Year Old Genius*.

Out of the blue, America's teen queen **Debbie Gibson** *wrote, produced and sang her way to the top.*

♦ The only British act to have two records in the UK Top 10 whilst she was still of school-age, was 15-year-old **Helen Shapiro** with her records 'Walkin' Back To Happiness' and 'You Don't Know' in October 1961.

♦ Welsh schoolboy **Aled Jones** dropped out of show business after scoring four Top 20 LPs in 1987 to concentrate on his 'O' level exams.

♦ American **Debbie Gibson** is the most successful teenage female singer/writer/producer in pop music history. She not only chalked up five Top 5 US hit singles and two Top 10 LPs (all of which she penned and produced as well as sang on) but she was also the first female teenager simultaneously to hold down the no. 1 single and album chart positions in the US. She did this in March 1989 with the single 'Lost In Your Eyes' and the album *Electric Youth*.

♦ The most successful year for young acts in the UK was 1988 when four separate teen acts hit the no. 1 spot. The acts were **Tiffany**, **Kylie Minogue**, **Bros** and **Glenn Medeiros**.

♦ The youngest female to top the UK album charts is Australian singer/actress **Kylie Minogue**, who did it with her LP *Kylie* in 1988, when she had just turned 20. The album went on to sell just under two million in the UK alone, making it not only the biggest selling debut album ever in Britain, but also the biggest seller ever by a female act. The video of the LP also shattered existing records by selling over 350 000 copies. Kylie, incidentally, has had the best start to a recording career in the UK of any act, having seen her first eleven singles go into the Top 4 with nine of them making the Top 2!

♦ Not many people can claim to have sold 15 million records before they reached the age of 21 but that's exactly what **Andy Gibb** did. The only Australian-born member of the singing Gibb brothers (**Bee Gees**) had a record three US no. 1 singles ('I Just Want To Be Your Everything', '(Love Is) Thicker Than Water' and 'Shadow Dancing' in 1977–78) with his first three releases and five other Top 20s, yet he managed only one Top 20 entry in the UK. Sadly, he died less than a decade later, in 1988.

THE NAME OF THE GAME

♦ Back in the first half of the century it was exceptional if recording stars or film stars used their real names. They frequently invented more interesting names for themselves. This practice continued into the 50s and early 60s but it has since become a rarer occurrence for an act not to use the name he/she was born with. There remain, however, those acts who still feel their own name would be a hindrance to their careers and choose a more exciting moniker . . .

STAGE NAME	REAL NAME
ADAMSKI	ADAM TINLEY
ADEVA	PATRICIA DANIELS
ADAM ANT	STUART GODDARD
DEREK B	DEREK BOLAND
ERIC B	ERIC BARRIER
BABYFACE	KENNY EDMONDS
BALTIMORA	JIMMY McSHANE
J.J. BARRIE	BARRIE AUTHORS
ROB BASE	ROBERT GINYARD
PAT BENATAR	PAT ANDRZEJEWSKI
DAVE BERRY	DAVE GRUNDY
CILLA BLACK	PRISCILLA WHITE
BARRY BLUE	BARRY GREEN
MARC BOLAN	MARC FELD
BONO	PAUL HEWSON
BOY GEORGE	GEORGE O'DOWD
ELKIE BROOKS	ELAINE BOOKBINDER
CAPTAIN SENSIBLE	RAY BURNS
VIKKI CARR	FLORENCIA BISENTA DE CASILLAS MARTINEZ CARDONA
CHER	CHERILYN La PIER
CHERRELLE	CHERYL NORTON
LOU CHRISTIE	LUGEE SACCO
TONY CHRISTIE	TONY FITZGERALD
ERIC CLAPTON	ERIC CLAPP
JESSI COLTER	MIRIAM JENNINGS
ALICE COOPER	VINCE FURNIER
ELVIS COSTELLO	DECLAN McMANUS
DANA	ROSEMARY BROWN
CHRIS DEBURGH	CHRIS DAVIDSON
KIKI DEE	PAULINE MATTHEWS
JOHN DENVER	HENRY DEUTCHENDORF
LYNSEY DE PAUL	LYNSEY RUBIN
STEPHANIE DESYKES	STEPHANIE RYTON
DADDY DEWDROP	RICHARD MONDA
DISCO TEX	JOE MONTANEZ JR
DIVINE	HARRIS MILSTEAD
SHEILA E	SHEILA ESCOVEDO
THE EDGE	DAVID EVANS
ENYA	EITHNE NI BHRAONAIN
DAVID ESSEX	DAVID COOK
ADAM FAITH	TERRY NELHAMS

STAGE NAME	REAL NAME
FALCO	JOHANN HOELZEL
FREDDY FENDER	BALDEMAR HUERTA
WAYNE FONTANA	GLYNN ELLIS
KENNY G	KENNY GORELICK
BOBBIE GENTRY	BOBBIE LEE STREETER
GARY GLITTER	PAUL GADD
GRANDMASTER FLASH	JOSEPH SADDLER
HUMANOID	BRIAN DOUGANS
JANIS IAN	JANIS FINK
ICE-T	TRACY MORROW
BILLY IDOL	BILLY BROAD
HARRY J	HARRY JOHNSON
L L COOL J	JAMES SMITH
JOAN JETT	JOAN LARKIN
JILTED JOHN	GRAHAM FELLOWS
TOM JONES	TOM WOODWARD
JUDGE DREAD	ALEX HUGHES
JUNIOR	NORMAN GISCOMBE
BIG DADDY KANE	ANTONIO HARDY
YA KID K	BARBARA KAMOSI MAOSO DUOGI
K.C. (& THE SUNSHINE BAND)	HARRY CASEY
KEITH	JAMES KEEFER
CHAKA KHAN	YVETTE STEVENS
ANDY KIM	ANDY JOACHIM
BEN E. KING	BEN NELSON
CAROL KING	CAROL KLEIN
PATTI LABELLE	PATTI HOLT
LEAPY LEE	LEE GRAHAM
KETTY LESTER	REVOYDA FRIERSON
GARY LEWIS	GARY LEVITCH
HUEY LEWIS	HUGH CREGG III
LIMAHL	CHRIS HAMILL
LISA LISA	LISA VELEZ
LOBO	ROLAND LAVOIE
JOHNNY LOGAN	SEAN SHERRARD
LIL LOUIS	LOUIS JORDAN
LULU	MARIE LAWRIE
ANNABELLE LWIN	MYANT MYANT AYE DUNN-LWIN
M	ROBIN SCOTT
MANFRED MANN	MANFRED LUBOWITZ
LITTLE PEGGY MARCH	MARGARET BATTAVIO
MARILYN	PETER ROBINSON
MARTIKA	MARTHA MARRERO
MEATLOAF	MARVIN LEE ADAY
FREDDIE MERCURY	FREDDIE BULSARA
GEORGE MICHAEL	GEORGIOS PANAYIOTOU
ZODIAC MINDWARP	MARK MANNING
DANNY MIRROR	EDDY OUWENS
EDDIE MONEY	EDDIE MAHONEY
NICOLE	NICOLE HOHLOCH

STAGE NAME	REAL NAME
GARY NUMAN	GARY WEBB
BILLY OCEAN	LESLIE CHARLES
OLIVER	WILLIAM SWOFFORD
MICA PARIS	MICHELLE WALLEN
BILLY PAUL	PAUL WILLIAMS
PEBBLES	PERRI McKISSACK
PLUTO	LEIGHTON SHERVINGTON
IGGY POP	JAMES JEWEL OSTERBURG
COZY POWELL	COLIN FLOOKS
WILL POWERS	LYN GOLDSMITH
PRINCESS	DESIREE HESLOP
STACY Q	STACEY SWAIN
REDHEAD KINGPIN	PAUL GUPPY
LOU REED	LOU FIRBANK
JOHNNY RIVERS	JOHNNY RAMISTELLA
ROACHFORD	ANDREW ROACHFORD
ROCKWELL	KENNEDY GORDY
JULIE ROGERS	JULIE ROLLS
BARRY RYAN	BARRY SAPHERSON
SABRINA	SABRINA SALERNO
SALT-N-PEPA	CHERYL JAMES & SANDRA DENTON
SHAKIN' STEVENS	MICHAEL BARRETT
SHANNON	BRENDA GREENE
SIOUXSIE SIOUX	SUSAN BALLION
GRACE SLICK	GRACE WING
WHISTLING JACK SMITH	BILLY MOELLER
BELOUIS SOME	NEVILLE KEIGHLEY
SONIA	SONIA EVANS
DAVID SOUL	DAVID SOLBERG
JIMMY SOUL	JIMMY McCLEESE

Taking pride in his Welsh roots **Tom** *swapped Woodward for* **Jones**.

Miss Patricia Holt *who labelled herself* **Patti Labelle**.

STAGE NAME	REAL NAME
DUSTY SPRINGFIELD	MARY O'BRIEN
SPRINGWATER	PHIL CORDELL
EDWIN STARR	CHARLES HATCHER
FREDDIE STARR	FREDDIE POWELL
CAT STEVENS	STEVEN GEORGIOU/YUSEF ISLAM
STING	GORDON SUMNER
JOE STRUMMER	JOE MELLOR
DONNA SUMMER	DONNA GAINES
AL B. SURE!	AL BROWN
SYLVESTER	SYLVESTER JAMES
SYLVIA	SYLVIA VRETHAMMER or ROBINSON (2 different hit acts)
TACO	TACO OCKERSE
TASHAN	THOMAS PEARCE
TAYLOR DANE	LESLIE WONDERMAN
JOE TEX	JOE ARLINGTON/JOSEPH HAZZIEZ
SUE THOMPSON	EVA McKEE
TIFFANY	TIFFANY DARWISH
TRACIE	TRACIE YOUNG
TINY TIM	HERBERT KHAURY
TONE LOC	ANTHONY SMITH
TINA TURNER	ANNIE BULLOCK
TWINKLE	LYNN RIPLEY
BONNIE TYLER	GAYNOR HOPKINS
VANGELIS	EVANGELOS PAPATHANASSIOU
BILLY VERA	BILLY McCORD JR
DON WAS	DON FAGENSON
DAVID WAS	DAVID WEISS
KIM WILDE	KIM SMITH
BRENTON WOOD	ALFRED SMITH
BILL WYMAN	BILL PERKS
TAMMY WYNETTE	VIRGINIA PUGH
YAZZ	YASMIN EVANS
YOUNG M.C.	MARVIN YOUNG
SYDNEY YOUNGBLOOD	SYDNEY FORD

Caesar and Cleo *or should that be* **Sonny and Cher** *– either way they are definitely all man and woman!*

♦ There are also many acts who, at some point in their careers, have worked or recorded under pseudonyms . . .

OTHER NAME WORKED/ RECORDED UNDER	BETTER KNOWN AS
ALLMAN & WOMAN	SONNY & CHER
BEACH BUMS	BOB SEGER
BEEFEATERS	BYRDS
BLUE RIDGE RANGERS	JOHN FOGERTY
BOTTOM LINE	DAWN
BILLY BRYAN	GENE PITNEY
BUDDIES	TOKENS
CAESAR & CLEO	SONNY & CHER
CARL & THE PASSIONS	BEACH BOYS
CHESTERS	IMPERIALS
DON CHRISTY	SONNY BONO
COEDS	TOKENS
COMPANIONS	TOKENS
CRAFTSMEN	JOHNNY & THE HURRICANES
CROSSFIRES	TURTLES
JIMMY DALE	JIMMY CLANTON
EDDIE DANO	EDDIE COCHRAN
DISTANTS	TEMPTATIONS
DUMBELLS	ROXY MUSIC
DUPONTS	IMPERIALS
FELIX & ESCORTS	YOUNG RASCALS
FOUR EVERS	FOUR SEASONS
FOUR SPEEDS	BEACH BOYS
ARTIE GARR	ART GARFUNKEL
GOLLIWOGS	CREEDENCE CLEARWATER REVIVAL
HARMONY GRITS	DRIFTERS
HENHOUSE FIVE	RAY STEVENS
IMPOSTER	ELVIS COSTELLO
INTERVALS	FIFTH DIMENSION
IVEYS	BADFINGER
JESUS LOVES YOU	BOY GEORGE
JILL & RAY	PAUL & PAULA
KENNY & THE CADETS	BEACH BOYS
KLARK KENT	STEWART COPELAND (POLICE)
JERRY LANDIS	PAUL SIMON
LUGEE & THE LIONS	LOU CHRISTIE
LARRY LUREX	FREDDIE MERCURY
BILL MARTIN	BILLY JOEL
MASCOTS	O'JAYS
MEN	HUMAN LEAGUE
OUTCASTS	GARY PUCKETT
PRIMES	TEMPTATIONS
PRIMETTES	SUPREMES
PAUL RAVEN	GARY GLITTER
RINKY DINKS	BOBBY DARIN
RONNIE & THE RELATIVES	RONETTES

OTHER NAME WORKED/ RECORDED UNDER	BETTER KNOWN AS
RUBBER BUCKET	GARY GLITTER
BILLY SHIELDS	TONY ORLANDO
SPORTS SECTION	HUEY LEWIS & THE NEWS
SUZY & THE RED STRIPES	LINDA McCARTNEY
TRUE TAYLOR	PAUL SIMON
TICO & THE TRIUMPHS	PAUL SIMON
TOM & JERRY	SIMON & GARFUNKEL
YELLOW BALLOON	JAN & DEAN

DON'T GIVE UP ON US

♦ **Jennifer Rush** holds the record for the most weeks on the UK chart before hitting the no. 1 spot. Her single 'The Power Of Love', which hit the top in its 16th chart week, went on to become the first single by a female act to sell a million in the UK.

*It was hardly a gold-rush, but thanks to the power of love American **Jennifer Rush** became the first female to have a million-selling single in Britain.*

♦ The oldest record on the US album chart to hit no. 1 was **Paula Abdul**'s *Forever Your Girl* which, in 1989, finally hit the top after 64 weeks climbing the chart. After a week at the summit it dropped down and then returned to the top in its 81st chart week. It was the first LP by a female to spend 50 weeks in the US Top 10 which was also longer than anyone else's debut album had remained in the Top 10. We can't close the record book on Miss Abdul without mentioning the fact that she broke *another* female record in the US when she spent 68 consecutive weeks in the singles Top 40 – a record **Connie Francis** had held for over 20 years.

♦ The record that spent the most weeks on the UK chart before getting into the Top 10 was **New Order**'s 'Blue Monday' which finally made that magic 10 in its 30th week on the Top 75. The runner-up, which took 23 weeks to make it, was **Grandmaster Flash**'s 'White Lines' in 1984.

♦ The longest wait from an act's first US album chart entry to its hitting the no. 1 spot is that of **Bonnie Raitt**, who first charted with 'Give It Up' in 1972 and finally topped the chart in 1990 with her Grammy-winning album *Nick Of Time* (which, incidentally, had slumped down to no. 119

It was a case of 111th time lucky for **James Brown.**

before news of its Grammy win sent it shooting up to the top – the first time such a thing had happened).

♦ **James Brown**, who is universally known as 'Soul Brother No. 1' and as one of the greatest performers of the 20th century, had to wait 30 years from his first recording 'Please Please Please' in 1956 to get his first UK Top 10 single with 'Living In America',which was his 111th US R&B chart entry!

♦ The record gap between an act's no. 1 hits on the UK chart was set by the **Righteous Brothers**, who first topped the chart in 1965 with 'You've Lost That Lovin' Feelin'' and returned to the top nearly 26 years later with 'Unchained Melody'. This broke the existing record set by the **Hollies** on 24 September 1988, when their 'He Ain't Heavy, He's My Brother' hit no. 1 – 23 years and two months after their only other chart-topper 'I'm Alive'.

♦ It was 16th time lucky in the UK for **Van Morrison** when, in 1990, his 16th chart album *The Best Of Van Morrison* gave him his debut in the UK Top 10, 25 years after his first chart appearance.

♦ It may seem to many record-buyers that overnight success is commonplace in the record industry. However, when the facts are carefully checked it becomes evident that it is quite rare for an act to score a hit with their first release, and some artists try for years before getting that important hit. In this category are **Clodagh Rodgers** (who was recording seven years before her first hit in 1969), **Hazell Dean** (who was recording for eight years before she hit) and **Lena Martell** (who waited 16 years from her first release). Another lady who had to wait a while for her first hit was **Kiki Dee**, who started recording in 1965 (at the same time and on the same label as **Elton John** first recorded) and did not chart until 1973, when she was on Elton's own **Rocket** label. **Nana Mouskouri** had to wait 17 years after her first UK LP chart entry to get her Top 20 singles debut – 'Only Love' in 1986.

♦ **Chris DeBurgh** had sold 10 million albums around the world and had released 23 singles in Britain before he had his first Top 40 hit in Britain with the no. 1 'Lady In Red'.

♦ For a long time it looked as if **Stevie Wonder** and **Elton John** would never top the UK singles chart with a solo release but Stevie finally did it in 1985 with his eighth US chart-topper 'I Just Called To Say I Love You', his 36th hit and Motown's biggest ever UK seller. Elton made it in 1990 with his 46th solo-charter 'Sacrifice'.

The family line-up of the **Osmonds**, *who took the world by storm in the 70s.*

◆ The single that has spent the longest time on the US Top 100 singles chart without making the Top 40 was 'If You Leave Me Now' by Manillan singer **Jaya**. It peaked at no. 44 and stayed in the Top 100 for 26 weeks.

◆ The album that has spent the most weeks on the US chart without ever getting into the Top 20 is **George Winston**'s *December*. The album first charted in 1983 and has returned to the chart at the end of every year since then, notching up a total of 174 weeks to date.

◆ It is most unusual for a record to stay long on the singles chart after reaching its peak, and the record for longevity after hitting its high spot goes to rapper **Young M.C.** and his recording of 'Bust A Move' in 1990, which remained on the US Top 100 for a further 25 weeks after reaching its peak of no. 7.

FAMILY AFFAIR

◆ Continuing the family tradition are **Michael**, **Nathan**, **David** and **Douglas Osmond**, the sons of **Alan Osmond** of the 70s supergroup the **Osmonds**. Like their father's group their first records (released in 1990) have failed to chart – the coming years will show if the **Osmond Boys** can duplicate the Osmonds' later success.

◆ The **Winan** family picked up three Grammy awards in 1990. **Be Be Winan** was voted Best Female Gospel Performance, **Ce Ce Winan** won an award for Best Male Gospel Performance and brother **Daniel Winan**'s choir won the award for Best Performance by a Gospel Choir.

◆ The most charted British siblings are the **Pearson** children who are known as **Five Star**. They were the first brother and sister group to score 20 UK hits and the first to top the UK album charts. Incidentally, they were also the first black British group to achieve either of these feats.

◆ It's not often that your godfather not only produces your records but also gives you a no. 1 hit, but that's exactly what happened to **Patti Austin**. Patti's godfather **Quincy Jones** was the man behind her US chart-topping duet with **James Ingram** 'Baby Come To Me' in 1982 – a single which took a record 23 weeks on the chart to reach the coveted no. 1 spot. Patti's godmother is the late top R&B/jazz/blues star **Dinah Washington**.

♦ When she topped the US chart in 1977 with 'You Light Up My Life', **Debbie Boone** made the **Foley/Boone** family the first to have three generations of chart-toppers. Her grandfather **Red Foley** had topped the chart in 1950 with 'Chattanoogie Shoe Shine Boy' and her father **Pat Boone** had several chart-toppers in the late 50s. Her mother **Shirley Foley** charted in 1950 singing with her dad on 'Rudolph The Red Nosed Reindeer'.

♦ The only other three-generation chart-toppers are the **Nelson** family. Born in 1935 grandfather **Ozzie Nelson** hit no. 1 in the US with 'And Then Some' and his son **Ricky Nelson** made the top with 'Poor Little Fool' in 1958 and 'Travelin' Man' in 1961. The trio was completed when Ricky's boys **Gunnar** and **Matthew**, known simply as **Nelson**, made the top spot in 1990 with '(I Can't Live Without Your) Love And Affection'. Amazingly, the single it replaced at the top – 'Release Me' – was by a second generation hit act **Wilson Phillips**. The female trio comprised **Carnie** and **Wendy Wilson**, the daughters of **Beach Boy Brian Wilson**, and **Chynna Phillips**, the daughter of **Michelle** and **John Phillips** from the **Mamas and Papas**.

♦ Oddly, the **Everly Brothers'** first hit – 'Bye Bye, Love' – was covered here by the **Beverly Sisters**! Phil Everly married his

record company boss's stepdaughter **Janet**, who was the daughter of **Jackie Ertel** of the 50s hit group the **Chordettes**, which made her Phil's mother-in-law!

♦ The most successful brother and sister act are **The Carpenters** with 17 US Top 20 singles and nine in the UK. They also hold the record for the longest gap between UK no. 1 albums for American acts – a gap of nearly 15 years between topping with *Horizon* in 1975 and *Only Yesterday* in 1990.

♦ The first siblings to top the US chart separately were **Michael Jackson**, who first did it with 'Ben' in 1972, and his sister **Janet Jackson**, who made it to no. 1 with 'When I Think Of You' exactly 14 years later. By the way, Janet was only just 20 when she hit the top, making her the youngest chart-topper since **Little Stevie Wonder** some 19 years before.

♦ **June Carter**, the country singer, is in the unique position of having her mother, aunt, uncle and her husband in the prestigious 'Country Music Hall Of Fame'. The first three were members of the **Carter Family** and her husband is **Johnny Cash**. It is also possible that more of her family may also be elected in time – her stepdaughter **Rosanne Cash** and her husband **Rodney Crowell** are two of country music's top acts at present. Rodney, in fact, is the first country act to have five consecutive country no. 1s from one album.

IT TAKES TWO

◆ Strangely, some top class singers have only managed to make the UK Top 40 when in the company of other artists. For instance **James Ingram** has hit in duets with **Michael McDonald** ('Yah Mo B There' in 1984), with **Patti Austin** ('Baby Come To Me' in 1983), **Linda Ronstadt** ('Somewhere Out There' in 1987) and as part of **USA For Africa** ('We Are The World' in 1985). James finally got a solo US Top 40 hit in 1990 with the no. 1 record 'I Don't Have The Heart', but unfortunately for him it did not give him his first UK solo hit.

◆ Two major US stars, **Michael McDonald** and **Patti Labelle**, who had many American hits both as solo acts and with their groups the **Doobie Brothers** and **Labelle**, scored their first ever UK Top 10 hit with their no. 1 duet 'On My Own'. Interestingly, they recorded their parts of the record and the video for it separately and never met until their first TV show to promote the hit. Other acts who needed assistance to make the UK Top 40 include:

◆ There have been some unusual duets over the years including **George Michael & Aretha Franklin**, **Cliff Richard & Janet Jackson** and **Placido Domingo & Jennifer Rush**, but probably the oddest combination was the 1977 teaming of **David Bowie** and a singer 40 years his senior – **Bing Crosby** – on a track that became a British Top 3 hit five years later – 'Peace On Earth – Little Drummer Boy'.

◆ The record number of duos in the UK Top 10 simultaneously is five, which occurred on 7th April, 1990. The five acts concerned were **Snap**, **Candy Flip**, **Erasure**, **Dave Stewart & Candy Dulfer** and **They Might Be Giants**.

HELP!

◆ The biggest-selling singles on both sides of the Atlantic in the 1980s were charity records and the proceeds went to help the starving people in Ethiopia. They were, of course, 'Do They Know It's Christmas' by **Band Aid** which sold over 3.5 million in the UK alone and 'We Are The World' by **USA For Africa** which sold

ARTIST	ONLY HIT WITH	HIT	YEAR
PATTI AUSTIN	JAMES INGRAM	BABY COME TO ME	1983
PEABO BRYSON	ROBERTA FLACK	TONIGHT I CELEBRATE MY LOVE	1983
DONNY HATHAWAY	ROBERTA FLACK	BACK TOGETHER AGAIN	1980
GRACE KELLY	BING CROSBY	TRUE LOVE	1957
WILLIE NELSON	JULIO IGLESIAS	TO ALL THE GIRLS I'VE LOVED BEFORE	1984
TAMMI TERRELL	MARVIN GAYE	(7 hits inc.) ONION SONG	1969
JENNIFER WARNES	JOE COCKER	UP WHERE WE BELONG	1983
KIM WESTON	MARVIN GAYE	IT TAKES TWO	1967

The biggest-selling single of the 80s was made by one of the biggest groups – the star studded **USA For Africa**

over 4.5 million in America.

♦ **George Harrison** organised and starred in 'The Concert For Bangladesh' in 1972, to raise money to help the people there. The $8.8 million raised by the show and from the worldwide smash hit album of the same name did not reach the people in Bangladesh until a decade later due to 'red tape' and legal problems.

♦ It is worth remembering that in the 'compassionate' year of 1985 many UK chain stores initially refused to stock the Ethiopian charity record 'We Are The World' by **USA For Africa** because they stood to make no profit from selling it. Interestingly, Wembley stadium originally said 'no' to hosting the 'Live Aid' show for the same reason.

♦ The most famous singing 'page 3' girl is **Samantha Fox**, but she was not the first one to sing on a no. 1 record – that honour belongs jointly to **Linda Lusardi** and **Maria Whittaker**, who were both in the group **Ferry Aid** whose charity record 'Let It Be' topped the UK chart in 1987. Incidentally, it was also the first hit record that the then unknown **Rick Astley** sang on.

♦ **Bananarama** was the only act to appear on both the **Band Aid** and **Band Aid II** chart-topping hits.

Bananarama *were really saying something when they were the only act to appear on both the Band Aid hits.*

♦ They say that charity begins at home and often that's the only place that charity records sell. Big UK charity hits that did not chart Stateside include:

HIT	ACT	UK CHART POSITION
'LET IT BE'	FERRY AID	1
'YOU'LL NEVER WALK ALONE'	THE CROWD	1
'WITH A LITTLE HELP FROM MY FRIENDS'	WET WET WET	1
'DRIVE'	THE CARS (re-issue for 'Live Aid')	4
'RUNNIN' ALL OVER THE WORLD'	STATUS QUO	17
'EVERYBODY WANTS TO RUN THE WORLD'	TEARS FOR FEARS	5
'DO THEY KNOW IT'S CHRISTMAS'	BAND AID II	1
'LIVING DOLL'	CLIFF RICHARD & THE YOUNG ONES	1
'HELP'	BANANARAMA & LA NA NEE NEE NOO NOO	3
'BEN'	MARTI WEBB	5
'YOU'VE GOT A FRIEND'	SONIA & BIG FUN	14
'FERRY CROSS THE MERSEY'	MARSDEN, McCARTNEY, JOHNSON, CHRISTIANS	1
'ROCKIN' AROUND THE CHRISTMAS TREE'	MEL (SMITH) & KIM (WILDE)	3

THE NAME GAME

♦ Over the years there have been literally thousands of recording acts with names that the public thought a little unusual, strange or downright funny. To narrow the multitude of such names down has proved to be the most difficult part of this book as one person's 'funny' can be another's 'clever', etc. It would have been easy to fill half the book with this type of trivia but we've narrowed it down to a selection of the most weird and wonderful, taken evenly from the last 35 years of UK and US acts.

ART ATTACKS
ATOMIC ROOSTER
ATTEMPTED MOUSTACHE
ATTILA THE STOCKBROKER
BENT FORCEPS AND THE PATIENTS
BLOOP GROUP
CAPTAIN FREAK AND THE LUNACYCLE BAND
CARNIVAL OF SLUSH
CHEERFUL EARFULS
CRISPY AMBULANCE
DASH FLASHER AND THE STREAKERS
DESPERATE BICYCLES
DICKIE DOO AND THE DON'TS
EGGS OVER EASY
FAR OUT, UNDERGROUND ACID ROCK FEET OF HARRY ZONK
FOREHEADS IN A FISHTANK
FUNKY WORM
FUR BIBLE
HALF MAN HALF BISCUIT
ICONS OF FILTH
IGNERENTS
IKE AND TURNER KORNER
LAUGHING GRAVY
LEATHER NUN
LIME SPIDERS

MEAT BEAT MANIFESTO
POOH AND THE HEFFALUMPS
POP WILL EAT ITSELF
RANDY PUMP AND THE GAS-O-LETTES
REVOLVING PAINT DREAM
SPELLING MISSTEAKS
THOSE NAUGHTY LUMPS
THROBBING GRISTLE
TINGLING MOTHERS CIRCUS
TRIPLETT TWINS
UNBELIEVABLE UGLIES
WIND BREAKERS
ZANY NO-TONES

♦ Some acts have leanings towards horror and madness:

ALIEN SEX FIEND
BETHLEHEM ASYLUM
CHRISTIAN DEATH
DAMNED
DEAD CAN DANCE
DEATH BY MILKFLOAT
DIE ELECTRIC EELS
DROWNING CRAZE
EYELESS IN GAZA
GHOST DANCE
HELLOWE'EN
LAWNMOWER DEATH
MORE-TISHANS
MILLIONS OF DEAD CHICKENS
MISSING PRESUMED DEAD
MURDER THE DISTURBED
MY LIFE WITH THE THRILL KILL KULT
NEW TOWN NEUROTICS
SCREAMING WILDMEN
SEVERED HEADS
SICKNICKS
SKELETAL FAMILY
STIFF KITTENS
STIFFS
STOCKHOLM MONSTERS
STRANGLERS
TERMINAL CHEESECAKE
THROW UPS

♦ Some acts simply ape their heroes:

AMERICAN BEATLES

BOOTLES
CARDBOARD ZEPPELIN
FEMALE BEATLES
JAPANESE BEATLES
RINGOS
SEX BEATLES

♦ It's not just groups who have 'interesting' names – there are many equally inventive solo artists:

ANNIE ANXIETY
BILL HORNY
BONGO BEAN
BOOTHOG PEFFERLY
BUBBA LITTRELL
CHESTER LESTER
CHIP FISHERS
CUCUMBER JACKSON
CURBY GOGGINS
CURLY WIGGINS
DADDY CLEANHEAD
DOC VITAMIN
DOUGIE THE DUDE
DUKE OF IRON
ED BANGER
FATSO BENTLEY
FLIP CARTRIDGE
GARLAND THE GREAT
GORDON THE MORON
HASH BROWN
HELMET BOY
HERMAN HITSON
HILLOUS BUTRUM
HONEY BOY HOMER
HOYT SCOGGINS
HURRICANE HARRY
JOE PUBLIC
JOHNNY CREDIT
JOHNNY PANCAKE
JOHNNY SOBER
JOHNNY WILDCARD
LAURA LOGIC
MAD DOG SHEFFIELD
MIGHTY POPE
MORRIS CHESTNUT
MR GOON BONES
NAPPY BROWN
OBIE DOBY
ORVILLE COUCH
POMONA JOE PENNYSWORTH

PRIMBROCK SKIGGS
RADIO BIRDMAN
RANDY GURLEY
RED HERRING
ROGER MUDSLINGER
RUSTY WELLINGTON
SKINNY DYNAMO
SMILING SAM
STICK HORSE HAMMOND
TANYA HYDE
TED BONK
TERRIBLE TOM
TNT TERRIBLE
TOAD FRALEY
WEE WILLIE
WINKY WISE
YOUNG BILLY BEAN

◆ Not forgetting these Americans with delusions of grandeur:

ANTHONY ARMSTRONG JONES
PRINCE CHARLES
PRINCE PHILLIP
MARK THATCHER

TRIVIA TIME

◆ The record time for recording and releasing an album is probably held by the official BBC album of the 1981 royal wedding of **Prince Charles** and **Lady Diana**. The album was available in the shops just two days after the event. By the way, there were many records released about the wedding, some serious, some humorous, but none of them charted.

◆ **Dick James**, music publisher for the **Beatles** and **Elton John**, recorded successfully as a singer with the **Stargazers** and **Anne Shelton**, as well as with the bands of **Geraldo**, **Cyril Stapleton**, **Stanley Black** and **Mantovani**. As a solo artist in the 50s, he had British hits with a cover of **Joe Valino**'s 'Garden Of Eden' and the theme song from the transatlantically successful TV show *Robin Hood*, on which he was joined by a group of schoolchildren headed by his young son Stephen, who is now a top music industry figure.

◆ Most pop fans know that **Michael Jackson**'s *Thriller* is the world's biggest selling record with over 40 million sales. However, even this total is five million short of the total copies of a vocal version of the McDonald's hamburgers menu pressed and given away as part of a $1 million competition in 1989.

◆ In the 50s, UK TV personality **Barry Cryer** unsuccessfully covered **Sheb Wooley**'s transatlantic novelty smash 'Purple People Eater' and **Eddie Fontaine**'s US rock 'n' roll hit 'Nothin' Shakin''.

◆ Two records featuring the 'singing voices' of dogs have charted in the UK. The first, in 1955, was recorded by a group of Danish dogs aptly named the **Singing Dogs**. The hit was a medley of 'Pat-a-Cake', 'Three Blind Mice', 'Oh Susanna' and (the most popular track) 'Jingle Bells'. In 1982 a team of British dogs called the **Wonder Dogs** made the Top 40 with 'Ruff Mix'!

◆ Many records have claimed to be the world's shortest single but discounting completely silent tracks (yes, they *do* exist) the record must surely be held by 'The Mistake' by **Dickie Goodman** (1974) on Rainy Wednesday Records which is less than 1 second long and is a very short extract from the B-side of the record, 'Energy Crisis '74'.

♦ 'The Twist', the song that started the dance craze, was first recorded by its composer **Hank Ballard** with his group **The Midnighters** in 1958 for Vee Jay records – who did not release it. With slightly amended lyrics, it first charted in 1959 when it was the B-side of Hank's 'Teardrops On My Letter' on the King label. Hank returned to the chart with it in 1960, as did a cover version by **Chubby Checker**. It was Chubby, of course, who topped the chart with it then and he took it to the top again in 1961 (the only record to go top on two separate occasions in the US), and in 1962 his version charted in the UK and started the craze off in Britain. Meanwhile, Hank's record label tried to remind the Twist-mad world who had set the ball rolling by releasing 'Thanks Mr Ballard For Inventing The Twist' by **The Escos** – it flopped. Incidentally, Chubby's 'Let's Twist Again' owed more than a little to Hank's 'Let's Go Again (Where We Went Last Night)'.

♦ In his early days, **Gary Glitter** (then performing and recording as Paul Raven) was known as a prótege of top comedian **Spike Milligan**.

♦ Singer **J.C. Mark** is proof that advertising sometimes *doesn't* pay. The Cybervoc Records artist, who has advertised regularly (about once every two weeks) in America's *Billboard* magazine since February, 1990, has not yet had even a hint of a hit.

♦ The only Christmas song to hit out of season was 'Little Drummer Boy'. The song entered the UK charts in two versions in February, 1959, one by the **Beverly Sisters** and the other by the **Harry Simeone Chorale**. It

remained on the chart until April. Simeone's version had hit Stateside before Christmas in 1958.

♦ The 'Tallahatchie Bridge' which was immortalised in the 1967 no. 1 by **Bobbie Gentry**, 'Ode To Billie Joe', collapsed in June, 1972.

♦ Radio personality **Jimmy Young** sang with **Ray Martin**'s band in the 40s and first charted on Polygon records in the 50s – making him one of the first 'indie' hit artists.

♦ **Betty Driver**, who plays Betty Turpin on Mondays, Wednesdays and Fridays in the much-loved UK soap opera *Coronation Street*, had a hit in 1949 with 'Monday, Tuesday, Wednesday'.

♦ British group **Doctor & The Medics** not only had their sole UK no. 1 with the **Norman Greenbaum** song 'Spirit In The Sky', but their name may also have been influenced by Norman as he originally recorded as Dr Norman Greenbaum.

Were **Doctor and the Medics** *unethical? Either way, after a healthy start they became a chart casualty.*

WHODUNNIT? – ANSWERS

WHODUNNIT? – ANSWERS

1. **YESTERDAY** (BEATLES/ MATT MONRO)
2. **THE WINNER TAKES IT ALL** (ABBA)
3. **GOLD** (SPANDAU BALLET)
4. **HIT THAT PERFECT BEAT** (BRONSKI BEAT)
5. **ALL AROUND THE WORLD** (LISA STANSFIELD)
6. **HAPPY BIRTHDAY** (STEVIE WONDER)
7. **WOMAN** (JOSE FERRER/ JOHN LENNON)
8. **IN THE COUNTRY** (CLIFF RICHARD)
9. **TRAGEDY** (BEE GEES)
10. **WE DIDN'T START THE FIRE** (BILLY JOEL)
11. **STARMAKER** (KIDS FROM FAME)
12. **STAR TREKKIN'** (THE FIRM)
13. **PLAY THAT FUNKY MUSIC** (WILD CHERRY)
14. **ALIVE AND KICKING** (SIMPLE MINDS)
15. **MONEY GO ROUND** (STYLE COUNCIL)
16. **THE NEXT TIME** (CLIFF RICHARD)
17. **BITS AND PIECES** (DAVE CLARK FIVE)